Ken Hudson is the author of best-selling books *The Idea Generator* and *The Idea Accelerator*, which have been published in Australia, France, the United Kingdom, Taiwan, Italy and Brazil, and distributed in the United States and India.

Ken has formed a breakthrough business called The Speed Thinking Zone, which is at the forefront of helping people unlock amazing results and thrive in a time-poor world.

He has worked with organisations as diverse as DuPont, Heinz, Qantas, Roche Pharmaceuticals, Dell Computers, PayPal and The Benevolent Society.

Ken was formerly a marketing director at American Express and has a PhD in Organisational Creativity. He can be contacted at

www.thespeedthinkingzone.com

'Speed Thinking is a great concept and Ken Hudson has made it accessible to everyone with simple practical tools that give us what we all need—the ability to do things faster without losing quality. Essential reading!'

Graham Winter, three-time Chief Psychologist for the Australian Olympic Team and author of *High Performance Leadership* and *Think One Team*

Praise for *The Idea Generator*

'Sixty practical tools come to the rescue of those starved of inspiration.'

Boss Magazine

'As an introduction to looking at your business in a new light, *The Idea Generator* will be hard to beat.'

Unlimited Magazine

'If you get stuck for good ideas—then Ken Hudson's new book *The Idea Generator* is for you.'

NZ Business

'This is an extremely user-friendly text that breaks down concepts with the help of clear diagrams and simple, real-life examples.'

Virgin Blue Magazine

'I have used Speed Thinking with my clients again and again. They love the idea that you can apply this to a consumer trend and quickly develop breakthrough brand and business-building concepts and opportunities.'

Paul Leinberger PhD, The Futures Company, and co-author of *The New Individualists*

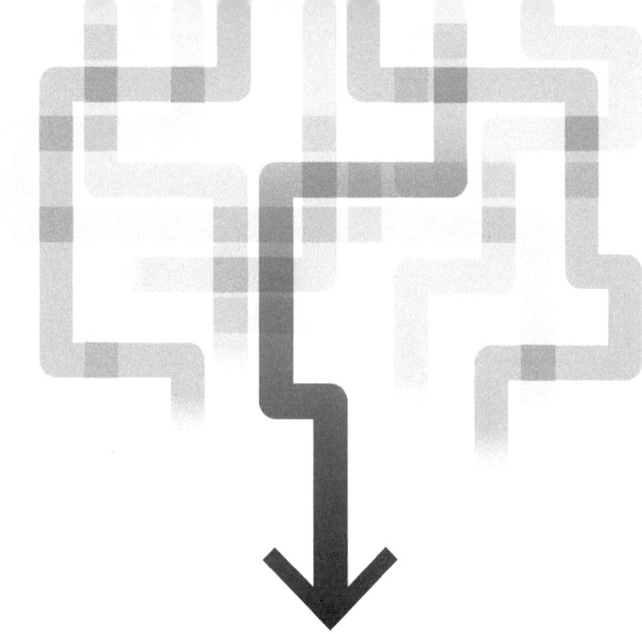

Speed Thinking

HOW TO THRIVE IN A TIME-POOR WORLD

Ken Hudson

ALLEN&UNWIN

First published in 2010

Allen & Unwin
83 Alexander Street
Crows Nest NSW 2065
Australia
Phone: (61 2) 8425 0100
Fax: (61 2) 9906 2218
Email: info@allenandunwin.com
Web: www.allenandunwin.com

Cataloguing-in-Publication details are available
from the National Library of Australia
www.librariesaustralia.nla.gov.au

ISBN 978 1 74175 995 2

Internal design by Simon Paterson
Set in 11/13 pt Adobe Garamond Pro by Bookhouse, Sydney

10 9 8 7 6 5 4 3 2 1

To Margot—my life-force

To Charlotte and Molly—my greatest joys

To Angela and Ian—thank you for believing in
and supporting this book

Contents

'Our brains can often decide well in seconds or minutes, depending on the time frame we set as appropriate for the goal we want to achieve.'

Antonio Damasio, *Descartes' Error*

INTRODUCTION

What is Speed Thinking?

Speed Thinking is a generative thinking system that enables any individual or team to deliberately and consciously accelerate the pace at which they normally think and act.

As this definition suggests, Speed Thinking aims to generate something of potential value quickly. It could be:

- a big, new range of ideas or solutions
- quicker decisions
- more innovative products that can be introduced faster
- a shorter, more productive meeting
- a better work/life balance.

Speed Thinking can be applied readily to everyday problem-solving, idea generation or decision-making. Business leaders and small business owners have also applied this new approach to how they conduct meetings, manage projects, service customers, develop new products and conduct focus group research. Speed Thinking is a new way of looking at the world which challenges the long-held belief that doing something quickly compromises quality. In this book I will suggest that thinking and working at an accelerated pace can not only improve quality but make you more productive and efficient.

In my experience, thinking quickly comes naturally. Our education system views thinking as a serious, step-by-step process that cannot be rushed. It is an irony, however, that in mathematics, for example, my youngest daughter is forever showing me faster short cuts. While I battle with my longhand way of multiplying and dividing, she already has the correct answer and has moved on to the next question. In the same way, I believe Speed Thinking offers business people and students the potential to accelerate their results and not get caught in the slow lane.

This is not to say that traditional thinking does not have its place. There will always be a role for a more measured, critical approach, particularly for momentous, long-term decisions—although there is some evidence that suggests the more difficult the decision, the more you should rely on your unconscious.[1]

Speed Thinking complements but does not replace the traditional thinking system. The ability to think either fast or slow, depending on the situation and time available, is priceless. Much like the Chinese concept of yin (slow) and yang (fast), the two thinking styles form a complete whole and are interdependent. For example, have you ever been struggling with a problem, then in an instant a new idea jumps into your head? Speed Thinking provides more energy, action and momentum than traditional thinking.

The central idea of Speed Thinking is that you can vary the pace at which you think depending on the situation, time available or your preference. This gives you more control at work and in general life.

Speed Thinking is a skill that can be learned by anyone and improved with practice. While some may be faster than others, in my workshops I have not found a person who cannot improve their ability to think more quickly and better given some practice, a new tool kit and encouragement.

Traditional thinking vs Speed Thinking

Traditional Thinking	Speed Thinking
■ Being correct	■ Just starting
■ Winning an argument	■ Creating movement
■ Based on critical analysis	■ Operates at the 'edge of the unconscious'
■ Cannot be rushed	■ Accelerating the pace reduces internal filtering of possible new ideas or solutions
■ Used only by professionals or the well educated	■ Can be used by anyone
■ Serious, rational, objective	■ Energising

Speed Thinking offers the best of both worlds—it adds 'structure' to your intuition and 'speed' to your analysis. It builds on Malcolm Gladwell's book *Blink*, in which he recounts stories of people making rapid-fire decisions based on their intuition honed after many years of experience in a particular area.[2] But Gladwell does not outline how this technique could be used by anyone, at any time. The process and tools of Speed Thinking, by contrast, can be learned by anyone of any age and used effectively almost immediately to help you and your team produce amazing results in time-pressure situations.

The insight behind Speed Thinking

After I completed a doctorate in organisational creativity, I established a creative thinking and innovation consulting business which I ran for five years. While working with managers from leading international brands, I noticed that they often produced outstanding work when I placed them under some time pressure.

Using this insight, I started reducing the amount of time I would give managers to solve a problem. There was little difference in output when I set a problem time limit at three hours rather than four. Even setting the time limit at two hours didn't appear to affect the results. If anything, participants became more focused, energised and creative.

An overview of the Speed Thinking system

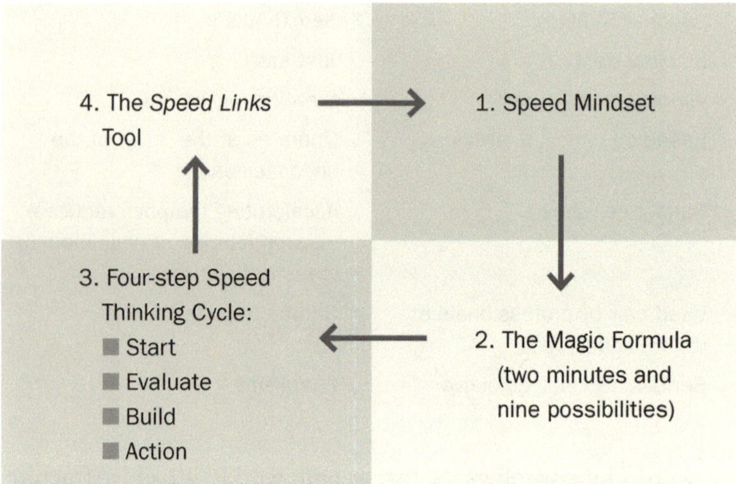

This gradual reduction in time led me to ask the question, *What is the smallest amount of time I could give an individual or a group to solve a problem?*

My answer? *Two minutes.*

Yes, that is correct—120 seconds to solve a problem. Through a process of trial and error, I came up with a two-minute time frame to which participants in my courses responded amazingly. Over literally hundreds of workshops I have fine-tuned this template and developed a Speed Thinking System consisting of:

- a two-minute, nine-possibility framework
- a Four-step Speed Thinking Cycle (Start, Evaluate, Build, Action)
- a new Speed Thinking tool called *Speed Links* that can be used in a seemingly unlimited variety of ways.

These features will all be discussed in the following pages as well as specific chapters on brainstorming ideas on demand, solving problems and making better, faster decisions. This approach can also be used in your personal life with immediate impact.

Who this book is written for

This book will appeal to anyone in business who is looking for a new way to solve their biggest dilemma—how to do more and more (e.g. work, sales, growth, targets, change, compete) with less and less (e.g. time, money, people). Working harder and longer is not sustainable. It can only lead to stress and burn-out. There is now a better way—it is called Speed Thinking and it will enable you to work faster, not harder.

Specifically, this book will be invaluable to any individual who wants to fast-track their success. If you have a tendency to procrastinate, this book can show you how to become a more confident decision-maker. If you are short of time and need to achieve a result quickly, Speed Thinking can help. Managers, team leaders, small business owners, coaches, facilitators, teachers, business consultants, trainers, human resource professionals, parents and students will discover that Speed Thinking is a vital new skill they can use to improve their results.

The biggest challenge facing everyone at work today

How to do more →

- Work
- Change
- Sales
- Grow
- Invest in myself
- Spend time with friends and family

With less

- Time
- People
- Money
- Energy
- Customer loyalty

The benefits of Speed Thinking

Some of the many benefits of Speed Thinking are:

- increased productivity
- reduced procrastination
- shorter, better meetings
- enhanced creativity and innovation
- quicker decision-making
- feeling more energised
- obtaining better study and exam results
- exercising your brain.

Research bites

Some fascinating research was conducted by Emily Pronin and Daniel Wegner at Princeton University which suggested that simply thinking more quickly can have a positive impact on your mood and energy levels. The research suggested that, just as people feel better after aerobic exercise, rapid thinking may induce a similar effect.

Source: Emily Pronin and Daniel Wegner, 'Manic thinking', *Psychological Science*, vol. 17, no. 9, 2006.

The structure of this book

Part 1 focuses on the theory and structure of Speed Thinking. Chapter 1 outlines the nine forces that are rapidly accelerating the pace of change today. It is this change in the environment that is forcing us all to adapt the way we think and act. We simply have to think more quickly to stay ahead. Viewed from this perspective, Speed Thinking is the perfect adaptation to a fast-moving, time-poor world.

Chapters 2 and 3 outline the basic mechanics of Speed Thinking, which is based on trying to create nine possibilities in two minutes.

This unlikely challenge forms the centrepiece, along with the Four-step Speed Thinking Cycle—Start, Evaluate, Build, Action.

Part 2 is built around the Speed Thinking tool that I have called *Speed Links*. Its unique visual design makes it easy to capture your initial thoughts then transform these into more powerful concepts as well as connecting these thoughts and concepts into an almost endless array of possibilities. Chapters 4, 5 and 6 focus on brainstorming new ideas, making better, faster decisions and solving problems in a fresh way. Chapter 7 outlines how you can use Speed Links to fast-track your success at work, at home or when you study.

There are many situations in life when you just have to think quickly. In the business world it could be when you need to adapt to a competitive move, make a quick decision or when you are asked for a response in a meeting. As a student it might be when you have to offer an opinion in a tutorial, or write an essay in an exam situation. Traditional thinking in these circumstances does not provide effective answers, as we shall see. We need a new approach—Speed Thinking is the answer.

Speed Thinking also helps you to get started. In the next two minutes, you can start to solve a problem, create nine new ideas or make a decision. Or you can keep worrying about it. This book will show you how to improve the efficiency of your thinking and create more time for yourself. Your time is your most precious resource. Don't waste the next two minutes. This is the start of your journey to a more productive and happier life.

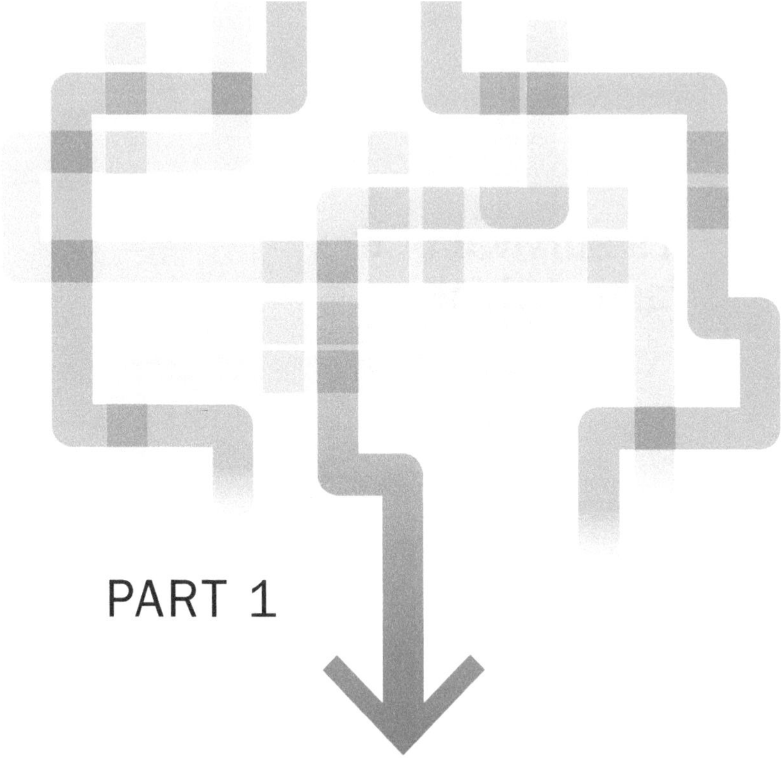

PART 1

The theory and structure of Speed Thinking

CHAPTER 1

It's survival of the fastest thinker

'What's dangerous is not to evolve.'

Jeff Bezos, CEO, Amazon, *Fast Company*, March 2009, p. 65

Over 150 years ago, English naturalist Charles Darwin published his seminal book *On the Origin of Species*, which became the foundation of evolutionary biology. He introduced the idea that populations evolve over generations as a result of natural selection. In the fifth edition of his book, he used the phrase 'survival of the fittest' (first used by English philosopher Herbert Spencer) as a short-hand way of describing natural selection, a process which suggests that the more 'fit' (in terms of its environment) an organism is, the better its chances of survival.[1] In essence, if the environment changes, you must adapt to survive.

I would like to borrow a little from Darwin and introduce a new concept called 'survival of the fastest thinker' to describe the way that we all have to adapt to thrive in an accelerating environment.

Speed is our new landscape. Rather than hoping for the world to slow down, we have to speed up our thinking to be able to cope in this new environment. As Vince Poscente suggests, 'the biggest reason we should speed up is to make time for meaningful experiences. Speed is not just the way to get more work done—speed is the secret to having time to do what we want'.[2]

We need to accept that the acceleration of all aspects of our work and life is here to stay. For most of us, our lives will only become faster, not slower. We need to adapt and evolve the way we think to this faster pace. The good news is that we already have all the equipment we need to adapt from a slow-paced world to an express one. But this will require a new mindset and thinking system.

The nine forces of acceleration

Let's start by highlighting and understanding the nine forces that are driving an accelerating environment.

1. IT'S A BROADBAND-PACED WORLD

Does anyone remember having a dial-up internet connection? It was slow, cumbersome and often unreliable. But now with broadband we can download or send a massive amount of information in the blink of an eye. Not only can we send information faster, but broadband enables new uses such as videoconferencing, streaming audio and video, interactive games and real-time voice services. The more we can do online, the more we expect to do and the faster we anticipate that it can be done. Perhaps the best technological example of this is Moore's Law, developed by Intel co-founder Gordon Moore in 1965. He predicted that the number of transistors on a chip would double about every two years. Forty-five years on, this is still the case.

More internet customers and connections around the world have also created a multiplier effect. If there is a riot in China or a flood in India, the rest of the world knows about it almost instantaneously. The more people that are online, the more the world is connected and the faster the flow of information and knowledge.

Added to this has been the explosion of text messaging. The increase in penetration of mobile phones in most countries and the convenience and lower cost of SMS have meant that people can communicate more quickly and easily than before. They have also created an expectation that when you receive an SMS message you must react to it quickly. Speed begets speed.

2. THE GROWTH OF SOCIAL AND PROFESSIONAL NETWORKS

Another recent development that has affected the pace of information and communication flows around the world has been the growth of social and professional networks. Think of the amazing expansion of Twitter, for example, or before this, Facebook, MySpace or the professional network LinkedIn. These network sites place emphasis on creating and maintaining connections, which means that the flow of information around your network can be completed as fast as you can type. Your network is connected to other networks and a speed multiplier effect is created. Your voice can literally be heard around the world in an instant.

We need to change our thinking to adapt to an accelerating environment

Faster environment

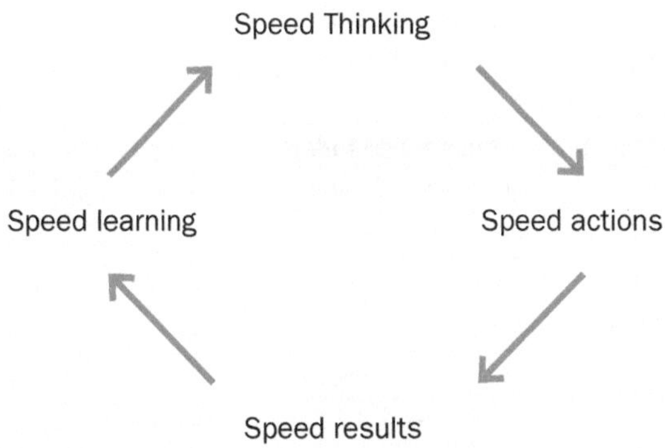

3. CUSTOMERS EXPECT FASTER AND FASTER SERVICE

Perhaps as a result of the lightning pace of the online world, customers are expecting their problems to be solved quickly in the offline world. Time is short, so the idea of lining up in a bank, insurance office, supermarket or post office no longer suits the customer today. In many instances, time to respond is the critical factor in how a consumer chooses to spend their money rather than the product range or price. Gone are the days when consumers were willing to wait. They want great quality at an affordable price—and they want it now. Increasingly, customers expect providers to use technology to offer a faster, better alternative (think of online banking, for example).

4. KNOWLEDGE AT YOUR FINGERTIPS

As I write this book, I am constantly checking my references and searching for new examples. Where do I go? Google and Wikipedia, of course. In the blink of an eye, I can find out the capital of Denmark (Copenhagen) or who wrote the novel *The Godfather* (Mario Puzo) or in what year Neil Armstrong and Buzz Aldrin landed on the moon (1969). In previous times, these questions might have resulted in a trip to a library or checking an encyclopedia.

Today, knowledge can be obtained and shared at a faster rate than ever before, and what you know needs to be constantly updated and challenged. Knowledge is expanding at an ever-increasing rate, just as the half-life of your own knowledge is decreasing.

Customers' expectations of service today

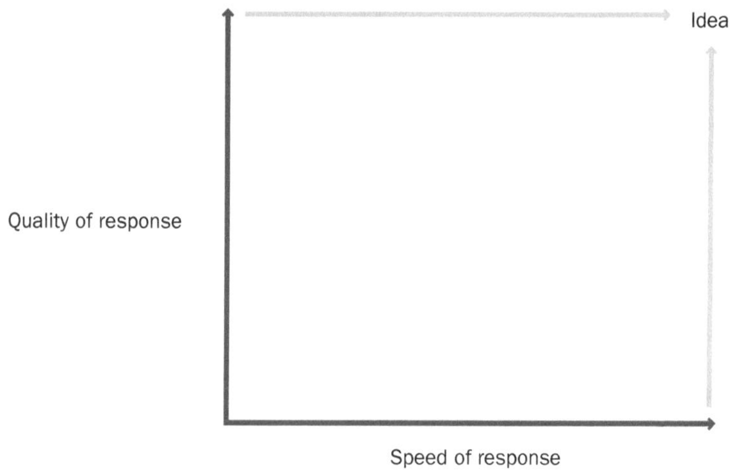

5. COMPETING ON SPEED

Do you know what *Time* magazine nominated as the invention of the year for 2007? Answer: the iPhone. This mobile phone developed by Apple has become the perfect metaphor for how business is adapting to and shaping a faster environment. The first generation iPhones were launched in 2007, the next generation iPhone 3G in 2008 and the latest iPhone 3GS was launched in 2009 (what does the 'S' stand for?—Speed).

Note how Apple is dramatically reducing its time to market. Every year there is a better and faster iPhone model. Each model is not only better than its predecessors but sets the standard for the rest of the industry in terms of style, cool, functionality and connectivity. Most of all, Apple is competing on speed—faster to market than its competitors, with a better product. This is the new way in which business has to compete in the future.

6. GENERATION Y

Our 18-year-old daughter is a flurry of activity as she manages to text her friends, call them the moment that something happens, listen to music, keep abreast of what is happening on her Facebook site and (seemingly) study all at the same time. This generation has grown up with multi-tasking and speed of response. Lightning-fast reflexes are needed to keep up with this sensory overload. As Don Tapscott observes, 'having grown up digital, [the Net Generation] expect speed—and not just in video games. They're used to instant response, 24/7. Video games give them instant feedback; Google answers their inquiries within nanoseconds. So they assume that everyone in their world will respond quickly too.'[3]

Why is speed important to:

An individual?

- Achieve more in a shorter time
- Do daily tasks more efficiently
- Free up more time for other pursuits.

A group?

- Enable common targets and goals to be met on time
- Create ideas and share knowledge more quickly
- Ensure decisions are not stuck in committees.

An organisation?

- Enhance client service
- Ensure profitability (time is money) and growth
- Enable the organisation to be more agile, respond to market changes and stay ahead of the competition.

Source: Responses from a group of partners and directors of an international management consulting firm that attended a Speed Thinking workshop in Sydney, Australia, 2009.

The implication of this emphasis on speed is that, as members of this generation move higher in an organisation or start their own business, they will want to keep thinking, working and living at this faster pace. Older business leaders will have to quicken up if they want to keep pace.

7. INCREASING WORKLOADS

With an eye on the bottom line, many companies are reducing the number of workers without reducing the amount of work. This means that increasing workloads are now the norm and this is occurring across all industries. For example, according to a recent survey among 1400 chief information officers (employing 100 people or more) in the United States, the greatest sources of workplace stress for IT professionals are:

- rising workloads (36 per cent)
- the pace of new technology (22 per cent)
- office politics (18 per cent)
- work/life balance issues (11 per cent).[4]

These factors have resulted in people working longer and harder, which causes more stress. This is not sustainable, so people are looking for a new way. We need a breakthrough to improve our productivity. Thinking and acting more quickly is one such way.

8. LACK OF TIME

At the same time people are being asked to do more and more, they have less and less—fewer people, smaller budgets and, most of all, less time. For many people, time has become their most scarce resource. It is not enough to manage time. Certainly, we can all be better at prioritising what is important, but what happens when we do not have enough time in the first place? We need to invent a new way—we need to create time. Accelerating the pace at which you think and work is a circuit-breaking idea that can help you create more time to invest in what is important to you.

9. PERFORM NOW OR ELSE

The last acceleration driver is perhaps the most stark. Managers and small business owners have to produce more with less time while trying to stay ahead of customer and technology changes. And at the same time, they must perform at a high level right from the start. There are no honeymoon periods anymore. New recruits have to deliver immediately. Anyone who is armed with the ability to think differently from others at a faster pace has a natural advantage.

> *'Information is no longer the bottleneck . . . thinking is.'*
> Edward de Bono, *New Thinking for the New Millennium*

We need a faster way of thinking to cope with an accelerating environment

These are the nine factors driving an accelerated work environment. Any one of these might have the effect of bringing about significant change, but taken together they represent a momentous shift in the way business is being conducted. A high-performance sport like swimming, for example, can illustrate this shift dramatically. In the 2009 Swimming World Championships, 43 world records were broken. This was due to a combination of dramatic advances in new technology (e.g. air-polyurethane swim suits), improved diet, training and competition. It was also a result of a different mindset. Seemingly untouchable barriers like Ian Thorpe's 400-metre freestyle record were shattered. Swimmers, like most other athletes, have evolved to become bigger, stronger and quicker. It is survival of the fastest.

The traditional thinking system has many advantages, but it has not been developed with a fast-moving environment in mind. We need an alternative to the slow, deliberate, conscious and analytical approach taught in our education system.

We have to abandon the 'one size fits all' mindset and develop an alternative thinking system that is faster, more generative and energising—one that can coexist with the traditional approach and provide a real choice depending on the situation, time availability

Speed tip

Our brain has a great capacity to 'chunk' information. This means that we can convey, learn and memorise a large amount of information by condensing it into small chunks. For example, instead of 'Let's develop a new product aimed at the kids' market', you could write 'Kids', which might convey all this information and associations. From a Speed Thinking point of view, this means you can save time (by not writing long sentences) and you can generate more ideas, more quickly.

and complexity of the problem. Imagine going for a run after work. You can stretch, walk, jog or sprint in any order depending on your mood, fitness level and how hard you want to push yourself. Research conducted by John Babraj has shown that low-volume, high-intensity interval exercise can have significant positive effects on your total workout.[5] Speed Thinking (like sprinting) can have the same effect—it makes your total thinking results better.

Are you a Speed Thinker?

Answer Yes or No to these questions:

- When you are criticised, can you quickly defend your position?
- Is it easy to see the mistakes in the thinking of others?
- Are you good at convincing others when you are right?

If you answered Yes to any of these questions, chances are your thinking is much slower than it need be.

Why? Because the traditional, critical thinking taught at school is judgemental. This is a slower way of thinking than Speed Thinking, which is about escaping from your point of view to a better one.

Source: Adapted from Michael Hewitt-Gleeson, *The School of Thinking*

One of the best ways I have found to illustrate the differences between traditional thinking and Speed Thinking is by way of analogy. Remember only a few short years ago when you had a film camera? You carefully studied your intended shot and then took your picture. But you did not take many because you then had to have your pictures processed some time later. This was both costly and time-consuming. To take good pictures took time and effort.

With a digital camera, you can take as many pictures as quickly as you wish. After each picture, you can immediately evaluate it. There is no real cost other than a few seconds of your time. Because of this it also means that you can take many shots of the same scene until you get just the right one. If you are not happy with your picture, you keep snapping away. With only a few lessons, the digital camera can be used by kids right through to the elderly. The entire process is fast, fun and interactive, and the pictures can be downloaded, manipulated and placed on a Facebook page, for example, for all to see within minutes.

In many ways, the digital camera represents Speed Thinking while the film camera is traditional thinking. With Speed Thinking there is no right or wrong approach, just an attempt to solve a problem or create an idea or make a decision quickly and effectively. If in a few minutes your solution does not lead anywhere, you can start again. All you have lost is two minutes.

This new way of thinking, like the digital camera, is a more practical and accessible way of adapting to a fast-paced world. So, the next time you are faced with a problem or decision, picture a digital camera rather than a traditional one and off you go.

Speed Thinking is a new way to look at the world. The *Speed Links* tool and the Four-step Speed Thinking Cycle outlined in the following chapters will open a new world of opportunities. Speed Thinking will help you to unlock your unique magic. You will no longer filter or place limits on what you can achieve. Most of all, it will encourage your authentic self to emerge.

Summary

In this chapter I have outlined the nine forces that are accelerating the environment in which most of us work, play and live. These forces are likely to become increasingly powerful and, because of their interconnectedness, will bring about even quicker change.

Traditional thinking, with its emphasis on reason, analysis and argument, has proven to be a successful thinking system over the years. However, it is based on thoughtful contemplation and deliberate assessment of various options. It is a slow system designed in a slow-moving environment.

We live in a different world—one that is fast, time-sensitive, constantly changing and more collaborative. We need another thinking system that can coexist with the traditional one. Speed Thinking offers you an empowering choice: you can choose how fast to think. My hope in writing this book is that you will try it and experience the difference. Then you can decide how and when to use Speed Thinking at work and in your life.

CHAPTER 2

Unlock two minutes of magic

'Speed will help you bypass your Censor.'

Julia Cameron, Mark Bryan and Catherine Allen,
The Artist's Way at Work

After I completed my doctorate in organisational creativity,[1] I established a creative thinking and innovation business called IdeaSpace. In the next five years I worked with many business leaders to help them create new products, solve problems and develop new revenue growth opportunities. During this time I developed a range of practical and effective creative thinking tools which I subsequently transformed into two books.

Typically, my work consisted of designing and then leading a series of one- or two-day workshops where the management team and I would go away to an external location and try to address a specific challenge or new opportunity. Although the businesses varied, over the years I developed a rough idea of how long each activity might take. One client, however, wanted to cram a two-day conference into one day, so I drastically reduced the amount of time for each activity. To my great surprise, the reduction in time and the subsequent accelerated pace of thinking seemed to have little effect on the team's outcomes. In fact, if anything, the managers seem to produce ideas and solutions or make decisions that were more original, fresh and unexpected than what they were used to.

This seemed counter-intuitive. How could people produce better results in a shorter time? Over a number of years and hundreds of workshops, I gradually reduced the amount of time that I gave clients to complete an exercise, and I kept achieving outstanding results. In these short bursts of activity, managers seemed more creative, energised and productive. Based on these observations, I asked myself what the shortest amount of time is that I could give an individual or group to start to solve a problem.

My answer? Two minutes!

It was the shortest amount of time that I could imagine and seemed the logical end point of reducing time and accelerating the pace at which managers could work. Managers were often amazed at what they could produce in two minutes. Again and again, over the next few years, I repeated this process and the results were the same. Participants in my workshops seemed to be able unlock their own two minutes of magic at will.

Nine time-pressure situations where Speed Thinking can help

1. You are asked for an immediate response in a meeting or presentation.
2. Your competitor has changed tack and you need to respond.
3. You have to make a quick decision.
4. You need to solve a customer problem ASAP!
5. You are procrastinating and need to get started.
6. You have a problem and require a range of new solutions in a hurry.
7. You are feeling low in energy.
8. You are frustrated with how long your meetings take.
9. You are faced with an essay-type exam.

But there was another piece to this puzzle. After a while, people became used to the shorter time and would then revert to a slower, more comfortable, business-as-usual thinking pace. To overcome this, I added a target of at least nine possibilities that participants had to try to achieve. The number nine emerged from my finding that for most exercises it was the highest number that anyone could achieve in two minutes. I thought that if one person could get to that figure then perhaps others could reach it as well. This created a stretch target that encouraged people not to filter (more on this later) and generated a sense of friendly competition. 'How many ideas did you come up with?' was a popular question in my workshops. Whatever the result (the average was 4–7 responses) became a benchmark that participants tried to beat the next time they were Speed Thinking. This goal of trying to improve their own results in turn created more energy and fun and less critical analysis.

The other advantage of having a target of nine possibilities is that it encourages managers to consider an array of surprising or left-field solutions. Left to their own devices, most people are happy to come up with perhaps three ideas, but when they are faced with the challenge of creating nine possibilities they are forced to use their imagination and offer up solutions that they might have initially considered silly or unworkable. Instead, these starting thoughts might just be the clue to solving a problem in an original way.

For example, I was working with an international management consulting company and the managing director responded to the challenge, 'What are nine things that make you smile?' His ninth response was an elephant. Asked what this meant, he indicated that when he was a kid his favourite activity was to go to the zoo and look at the elephants. This image transformed the MD from a serious, rational management consultant into a big kid with a huge smile. We then followed this with the task 'What are nine things our business could do to improve its client service?' Using the elephant as a metaphor, the MD realised that his business was incredibly heavy handed in the way it dealt with its clients.

Research bites

Some fascinating research by Sian Beilock, Bennett Bertenthal, Annette McCoy and Thoma Carr suggests that, with well-learned skills (in this case, above-average golfers putting a golf ball), a faster execution can actually enhance performance (i.e. their putting improved by 25 per cent).

This is the opposite of previous research that suggests there is a trade-off between speed and accuracy.

Source: Sian Beilock, Bennett Bertenthal, Annette McCoy and Thoma Carr, 'Haste does not always make waste: Expertise, direction of attention, and speed verses accuracy in performing sensorimotor skills', *Psychonomic Bulletin & Review*, vol. 11, no. 2, 2004, pp. 373–9.

In this example, the managing director had gained an extraordinary insight about his business precisely because he had not self-filtered a response as he might have done using traditional thinking. A left-field, initial thought might just be the key needed to unlock a new solution. The magical nine target forces you not only to think quickly but also creatively.

The challenge of generating nine responses is also consistent with our understanding of the capacity of our short-term memory. Estimates vary, but it is generally believed that our capacity is seven plus or minus two.

The basic mechanism of Speed Thinking is the combination of two minutes and nine possibilities. These two factors work in a synergistic way which enables most people to accelerate their thinking. Speed Thinking provides a structure in which people can create, solve or decide at an express pace. This two-minute, nine-possibility template, together with the four-stage Speed Thinking Cycle (Start, Evaluate, Build, Action) and the *Speed Links* tool (both of these are discussed in detail in later chapters), forms the basis of the Speed Thinking System.

The Speed Thinking experience

What does it feel like to start solving a problem in such a short period of time?

Without hesitating, in the next two minutes answer the question 'What are nine things you feel passionate about?'

1.

2.

3.

4.

5.

6.

7.

8.

9.

How did you go? How many initial thoughts did you have? What did it feel like?

What did it feel like when you were Speed Thinking?

1. Nervous
2. Happy
3. Clarity
4. Enlightened
5. Fun
6. Anxious
7. Playful
8. Electricity
9. Energetic

Source: Responses from a Speed Thinking workshop with a management team from a large service business

Now you have some idea of the concept of Speed Thinking. There are no right or wrong, good or bad thoughts. This is quite different from traditional thinking, which is predicated on having a single correct position and being able to defend it from attack by others. With Speed Thinking, this burden is relaxed at the initial stage of the process before your thoughts are evaluated and built into a stronger idea, solution or decision. The emphasis is on just letting go and not filtering.

The aim is to unlock your initial, raw responses. Your more developed solutions will emerge through an iterative process of starting, evaluating, building and acting (see Chapter 3). Notice that I am using the word 'thought'. Speed Thinking, as the name implies, is still a thinking rather than an emoting process.

The other feature of Speed Thinking is the emphasis on just starting and, unlike traditional thinking, there is no appropriate or inappropriate place to start. Just get going. Starting creates movement, energy and a positive cycle. Because of the limited time available, the process of starting is easy with Speed Thinking. People with a tendency to procrastinate find this empowering because they are not weighed down by whether to act or not; they simply must start. To reach the end of the race requires starting. The only real failure is a failure to start.

To achieve the nine initial thoughts in two minutes requires absolute focus. Speed Thinkers become totally absorbed in the challenge. They are right in the moment, with no anxiety about the past or the future—the focus is on what is happening right now. This enables people to be more playful, alive and authentic. New ideas, solutions or decisions pour out in a stream of consciousness. It appears that participants in my workshops enter their own *zone* of high performance, much like sportspeople who for the briefest of moments can do anything they want, seemingly at will.

> *'Our right brain kicks into high gear when we are doing things in the present moment—like performing, improvising or playing by ear.'*
>
> Jill Bolte Taylor, *My Stroke of Insight*

Sportspeople often call this mindset being 'in the zone'. As former Australian Olympic team psychologist Graham Winter explains, the zone is the ideal performance state. It is the state of mind and body in which we perform at, or near to, our best. It is easily recognised in sport, but is relevant to all areas of performance, such as business, the performing arts and medicine.[2] Speed Thinking enables you to enter your own high-performance zone at will, whenever you need to, either at work, home or study.

Another way of describing the Speed Thinking experience is as being in a flow-like state. Psychologist Mihaly Csikszentmihalyi has developed the concept of 'flow', in which a person is fully immersed in what they are doing. He describes the components of flow as:

- having clear goals
- concentrating and focusing
- a loss of self-consciousness
- direct and immediate feedback
- balance between ability and challenge
- intrinsically rewarding activity
- absorption in the challenge.[3]

Let's consider these features in turn. Speed Thinking has clear goals (e.g. nine thoughts in two minutes), there is a deep focus, people are too busy to worry what others think of them, there is immediate feedback and with practice there is a balance between the challenge and your ability. People also love the idea that thinking can be quick and it can be fun. This ability to enter your high-performance zone or achieve a flow-like state can have an important impact on your own and others' productivity and enjoyment at work. It partly explains the findings of researchers Emily Pronin and Daniel Wegner, who have found that thinking quickly—what they call 'manic thinking'—can give you an instant lift in mood.[4]

> *'Even in the most difficult situations, when you focus on what is right in the present moment, it makes you happier and gives you the needed energy and confidence to deal with what is wrong.'*
>
> Spencer Johnson, *The Present*

The goal of Speed Thinking for adults and kids is to create a safe environment where people can unlock often hidden ideas and solutions by accelerating the way they think. The aim is to enjoy the ups and downs of the Speed Thinking experience, much like a roller-coaster ride, and uncover capabilities in yourself that you never imagined.[5]

Five key reasons why Speed Thinking works

1. IT PROVIDES AN INTENSE FOCUS

We live in a short-attention-span, multi-task world. We all seem to be forever trying to do a number of things at once. We believe we can reply to an email at the same time as answering the phone as well as listening to a conversation near our desk. The reality is that we have become faster at processing each one of these tasks, which gives the impression that we are doing a number of tasks simultaneously.[6]

Speed Thinking, with its small time frame (i.e. two minutes) and challenging target (i.e. nine possibilities), tends to focus the mind on the specific task at hand. It is as though we have forgotten what it is like to really concentrate on something for a period of time. This means that we are not easily distracted as we enter a 'flow-like' state and that, by doing so, we can create better results than if we are jumping from one task to another. It is a paradox, but to work faster we need to concentrate on one thing at a time.

> » *'Fear is our greatest psychological obstacle—it stifles our motivation and can keep us stuck in unhappy situations for years.*
>
> *Common fears include the fear of failure, fear of disapproval, fear of making the wrong decision, fear of change and fear of stress and hassles.'*
>
> Sarah Edelman, *Change Your Thinking*

2. YOU DO NOT LIMIT YOURSELF

During my training programs on creative thinking I noticed that one of the biggest barriers for people was their own internal voice, which constantly told them that they were not creative. I found this critical inner voice intriguing as it surfaced again and again. For example, you cannot do this because you are not smart enough or experienced enough or educated enough. As professional golf teacher Bob Rotella notes, 'the little critic inside your head influences performance in two ways. He can affect your self-image and self-confidence in the future. And he can have an immediate and destructive impact on your ability to perform in the present'.[7]

Speed Thinking provides a simple solution to your self-limiting internal voice. You are simply too busy to worry about what that voice is saying. You are more consumed with meeting the two-minute challenge. Accelerating your thinking can reduce your destructive inner voice and help you achieve better results. Performance coach Timothy Gallwey observes, 'I found that when I could quieten Self 1 (my judgemental inner voice) and let Self 2 (my inner potential) learn and play without interference, my performance and learning rate improved significantly.'[8]

3. YOU DO NOT WORRY ABOUT OTHER PEOPLE'S EXPECTATIONS

In a similar vein, one of the biggest barriers to continued high performance is that we spend so much time worrying what others think of us. It could be that we are trying to live up to what we believe are the expectations of parents, partners, friends or a boss. Speed Thinking bypasses your anxieties because you are too involved to worry about what other people may be thinking. Without these self-imposed limitations, you can think and act in a more original and authentic way.

4. YOU OPERATE AT THE EDGE OF YOUR UNCONSCIOUS

A recurring feature of Speed Thinking is how participants are sometimes amazed by their initial thoughts. They often say, 'This just came to me, I am not exactly sure what it means'. Because of the speed at which they are operating, they cannot use their conscious mind or logic or critical thinking. They have to rely on something else, which I believe is their unconscious. In my thinking I am heavily influenced by Chaos and Complexity Theory. In any complex adaptive network (like our mind) there is a dynamic space called 'the edge of chaos'. Some of the general features of this space include the following:

- Complicated behaviours occur, e.g. improvisational music.
- Few rules exist.
- Work is required to maintain a balance on the edge of chaos.
- Surprise exists.
- Mistakes occur but there is also a quick recovery.[9]

I believe that when we are Speed Thinking we operate at the 'edge of our unconscious'. This is a dynamic space between our conscious and our unconscious. We can sometimes access new ideas, solutions or connections that our unconscious mind has been playing around with.[10] Rather than thinking about conscious and unconscious as an either/or situation, I believe that there are moments when these two interact and that Speed Thinking is one such time.

We are gradually gaining a more accurate picture of how our brains work. Recent work by Kalina Christoff at the University of British Columbia in Vancouver, for example, suggests that 'mind wandering (e.g. daydreaming) is a much more active state than we ever imagined'.[11] I believe that when we are Speed Thinking we are able to tap into the unique creative force we all possess.

Operating at The Edge of your Unconscious (Your Speed Thinking Zone)

Conscious	Emergent	Unconscious
Left brain	Flow	Right brain
Order and rules	Peak	Random
Structure	Spontaneous	Unstructured
Patterns	Trust	Freedom
Language	Focus	Visual
Judge	In the moment	Imagination
	'Feels good'	
↓	↓	↓
Self-imposed limits	**Breakthroughs**	**Your potential**

> *'Do you ever go up to a tee and say, don't hit it left, don't hit it right? That's your conscious mind.*
>
> *My body knows how to play golf. I've trained it to do that. It's just a matter of keeping my conscious mind out of it.'*
>
> Tiger Woods

5. IT CREATES A SAFE SPACE

Speed Thinking works particularly well in a group setting because it reduces internal filtering and external expectations, and creates a safe space for participants to play, collaborate and improvise. I have noticed that people are far more open to a new idea or solution than in a normal, more formal setting and feel better when they are Speed Thinking, so there is an explosion of energy in the room and a sense of jointly exploring opportunities.

Summary

In this chapter I have described the twin building blocks of Speed Thinking—the two-minute time frame and the nine-possibility challenge. These two principles work in a synergistic way to help most people to think and work faster. By doing so, the quality of the results can be enhanced because you are less likely to limit your performance by listening to your internal critical voice or worrying about the expectations of others.

By trying to reach the nine-possibility challenge in two minutes, you are forced to focus without distraction, which can lead to a 'flow'-type experience. This higher performing state can result in greater creativity, productivity and enjoyment.

In a time-poor world, every minute counts. Speed Thinking will help you unlock your magic to the world.

CHAPTER 3

The Four-step Speed Thinking Cycle

'Tell me and I will forget, show me and I may remember, involve me and I will understand.'

Confucius

There is more to Speed Thinking than unleashing two minutes of magic. This provides the energy, but you still need a structure. The four steps outlined in this chapter provide a way of structuring your intuition. These four steps enhance the rigour of this type of fast-paced thinking and ensure quality outcomes in time-pressure situations.

The Four-step Speed Thinking Cycle

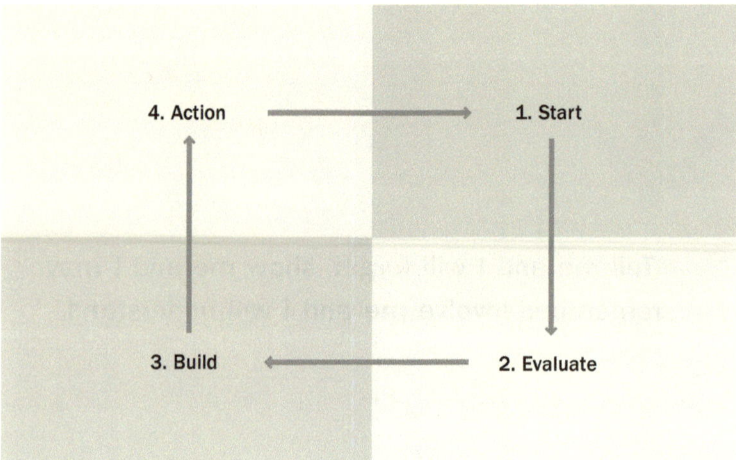

Before we look at each stage of the Four-step Speed Thinking Cycle (Start, Evaluate, Build, Action) in detail, it is important to highlight a number of key features.

1. IT IS AN INTEGRATED SYSTEM

The Four-step Speed Thinking Cycle has been designed as an integrated system. This means that each step should be considered as part of a bigger whole. To obtain the full impact of this accelerated approach, it is necessary to complete each of the four steps. As each stage is connected and interdependent with the other stages, if you change one part of the system you change all of the system. For example, it would be a wasted opportunity if you developed a range of initial thoughts quickly then spent the next five days evaluating these possibilities. This would kill any momentum you had created. This system-like quality is quite different from the linear, cause-and-effect nature of traditional thinking.

2. IT BUILDS ON ITS OWN FOUNDATIONS

The cycle—Start, Evaluate, Build, Action—has been designed through trial and error in this particular order. You start, then quickly evaluate a possibility, then try to build it into a bigger idea or solution. You then develop an action plan to implement or test the new concept. These four steps should be thought of as a general guideline rather than a rigid structure. The aim of Speed Thinking is to continually move to a solution, decision or breakthrough idea. It is a practical process where there is no right or wrong way to use the four stages. Hence you can vary the process to suit your needs. You could, for example, Start then evaluate, then build a new concept, then go back to the Evaluate stage if this concept is not leading you to a fertile new solution. Or you could jump forward to the Action stage.

Because each stage of the Four-step Speed Thinking Cycle takes two minutes, the most you can ever risk is eight minutes (if you complete all four stages). There is enormous upside when this process works, but very little downside. If an area is unproductive, you simply go back to the preceding stage and start again. You can elect to stop the process when you feel that your problem is solved or you have a fresh idea or have made a decision.

3. IT IS BASED ON AN EXPERIENTIAL LEARNING APPROACH

Speed Thinking is a powerful form of learning based on doing rather than reading or being lectured. Much like learning to swim, you eventually have to jump in the water and splash around. Ideally, this should be in the shallow rather than the deep end!

In my workshops I describe the concept only briefly, moving quickly into a Speed Thinking experience. Only by doing Speed Thinking can you truly understand its power.

>> *'The most powerful learning comes from direct experience.'*
>
> Peter Senge, *The Fifth Discipline*

4. IT IS FUN

This is perhaps the most surprising aspect of Speed Thinking for most people. Fun and thinking are not often linked. Teaching people to think, for most of our educators, is a serious business. Critical thinking relies on analysis, the use of logic, a belief that there is a best or correct answer, that it should be conducted in a measured, time-consuming way and, above all, that it should be objective. It is commonly seen as what separates the most intelligent from the rest.

Speed Thinking, with its emphasis on starting and moving, is fun, exploratory and playful. I have found that everyone can be taught to do this in an interactive, engaging way that creates rather than saps your energy.

On a recent trip to Singapore, 'fun', 'interactive' and 'collaborative' were the words most participants used to describe my Speed Thinking workshops. By making it fun, people can play, take risks and make mistakes in a safe environment. As biologist Brian Goodwin observes, 'it is in play that we see the richest, most varied and unpredictable set of motions of which an animal is capable'.[1] Somehow, when we grow older we often lose this ability to play and smile at ourselves. Speed Thinking allows us to do this again, and for most of us it is a magical feeling.

>> *'Serious play is not an oxymoron; it is the essence of innovation.'*
>
> Michael Schrage, *Serious Play*

Step 1: Start

For most people, starting a new project can be hard. I remember fifteen years ago agonising over whether to enrol in a part-time, MBA program. I found all sorts of reasons not to commence. Some of these reasons made more sense (e.g. the impact on my family) than others (e.g. who needs an MBA anyway?). Every year the enrolment period would come and go. I would procrastinate and the opportunity would pass me by. Finally, one of my work colleagues suggested I just send off the application, then decide later. I was fortunate enough to be accepted and, before I knew it, I was in my first class listening to the lecturer and wondering what I'd made such a fuss about.

With Speed Thinking, the emphasis is on taking the first step—ignoring all the reasons not to act and just starting. But this simple step is often the hardest. I was intrigued by why most of us find it difficult, so I asked a group of managers in a large organisation in one of my workshops. Their nine most common reasons *not* to start a project are given below:

1. Not enough time
2. No money
3. No interest, motivation or passion in the task
4. Lack of the necessary skills, experience or knowledge
5. Fear of failure
6. Commitments to other projects
7. No other people to help them
8. No deadline or goal
9. Low energy levels.

Which of these reasons do you most relate to? They all sound valid on one level, but do we use these reasons as an excuse to rationalise why we never seem to start?

To start any new project can be both motivating and energising. It is also the first sign of innovation. As lateral-thinking expert Michael Hewitt-Gleeson notes, 'to start is the fundamental creative act'.[2] Without someone starting something, somewhere, nothing ever happens. Nothing ever changes. It has been suggested, for example, that the modern-day civil rights movement in the United States was started when Rosa Parks refused to follow the bus driver's order that she give up her seat to a white passenger.

The starting point with Speed Thinking typically is to create nine new ideas in two minutes or nine solutions or nine aspects of a decision. The aim is to just get going as quickly as you can. With Speed Thinking there is no right or wrong place to start. The only mistake a person can make is not starting. You can keep worrying, analysing or procrastinating—or you can start. As stress consultant

Nine ways you can start

1. Write the first paragraph of the book that you have always dreamed of writing.
2. Ring up someone you have not heard from for a while.
3. Make five new prospect sales calls this morning.
4. Design a quick prototype of a new product and show it to some people.
5. Ask your boss how you are performing.
6. Set yourself a new goal for the week.
7. Go for a walk right now.
8. Sit down with your kids when they do their homework.
9. When you get stuck in your business, ask yourself what customer problem your product or service solves.

and best-selling author Richard Carlson suggests, 'happy people understand that the name of the game is to enjoy life rather than to think about it'.[3]

The important point at this stage is to continuously remind yourself that your aim is to create a range of different possibilities or initial thoughts. It is only in the following stages that these will be evaluated, built and actioned.

Step 2: Evaluate

One you have created a range of potential solutions or ideas, the next step is to do a quick evaluation. The aim here is not to conduct a protracted and agonising debate over the relative merits of each possibility but to simply evaluate them in two minutes.

People are often amazed at how quickly they can evaluate when they are asked to do so in a short period of time. In a blur of activity, they can form a coherent rationale for ranking options in minutes. I suspect that they can do this because they are using both the left and right sides of their brain. Typically, business people only use left-brain considerations (e.g. will it save money? is it on strategy?), which can lead to procrastination as various financial analyses go back and forth. However, as we will discuss in Chapter 5, effective decision-making is a combination of head and heart.

Nine ways you can evaluate an idea or solution in two minutes

Score each option from 1 to 10 in two minutes.

1. How passionate do you feel about the idea?
2. How quickly can you test a new solution?
3. How easy is the idea to communicate?
4. What is the profit or sales potential of the idea?
5. How different is your solution from what exists in the market?
6. How simple is the idea?
7. Can we do it?
8. Is this new idea consistent with our brand or business image?
9. Is there a gap in the marketplace for this solution?

The ability to make a quality evaluation quickly is reflected in research by psychologists Timothy Wilson and Jonathan Schooler, who asked college students to judge a range of strawberry jams and compared their results with the findings of experts. The students' preferences were not very different from those of the experts. However, when the students were asked to analyse (left-brain activity) their responses, their results varied significantly from the experts' results.[4] It seems that over-analysing a range of options may mean that people focus on criteria that are not significant. I have found that, when you encourage people to quickly evaluate their options, they respond with enthusiasm.

One powerful way of evaluating is to use what I call the Passion Meter. This is a quick way of measuring how passionate you feel about a particular option or initial thought. Passion, I believe, is the most important aspect in making and implementing a decision. Passion gives you energy, which is what is needed to get anything up and running. If an option makes rational, logical or financial sense, it still will flounder without someone somewhere saying, 'give it to me, I will give it a go and make it happen'.

In the evaluation process, after you have created a number of options ask yourself: 'How passionate do I feel about option one on a scale of 1 to 10?' (1 being indifferent, 10 being you love the idea or solution). Then repeat for option two, three, and so on. It is important just to score the ideas and not to rank these at this stage. In two minutes you will have sorted the options according to passion. Go with the highest scoring options. You will have a greater chance of making it a success and, because you care about it, you will do better work.

Step 3: Build

The third step in the Four-step Speed Thinking Cycle is to focus on the highest evaluated option and then try to make this initial idea or solution nine times better. Ideas or solutions are never born perfect. They need to be nourished and expanded. The Start step gets your initial thoughts out. The Evaluate step takes these thoughts and tries to identify the ones with the most potential. The Build step tries to realise this potential by transforming a raw idea into a workable concept. As with all the steps, if the initial highest evaluated option does not work out as expected, you can go back in the cycle to the previous step and select another thought and work for two minutes on this.

Nine questions to build a better idea or solution

1. Can the idea make the user experience delightful?
2. Can the idea be made simpler?
3. Can the idea generate more revenue?
4. Is there an online version you could develop?
5. Can the idea be made more original?
6. Can the idea save more money?
7. Is the solution environmentally friendly?
8. What would excite the retailer about this idea?
9. Can you develop a premium version?

This step is most concerned with enhancing an initial thought and can be completed by an individual or with a partner. You might both do the Start step individually and then complete the Evaluate, Build and Action steps together. This process combines the magic of the individual with the strengths of working with others.

The continued emphasis on speed at this stage has a number of advantages. It maintains the sense of momentum and progress and encourages participants to be more open and willing to consider new ideas rather than slipping into a critical, judgemental role. Because there is little time, people do not listen to their own critical voice, nor do they become critical of others. Many people are surprised at how receptive others can be in such a short period of time. The other advantage is if, after two minutes of totally focused effort, you cannot build a better concept, then perhaps it is time to move on to another idea. In Speed Thinking the emphasis is on trying to reach a result as quickly as you can without defending or arguing the merits of your position.

Step 4: Action

The Four-step Speed Thinking Cycle is concerned with making something happen. It is not a clever, legal argument aimed at trapping an opponent, nor is it concerned with following the rules of logic. The primary aim is to create a breakthrough idea, solve a problem or make a quality decision quickly. It makes sense, therefore, for the final step to be action-oriented.

>> *'Motivation is movement.*

> *By taking action, by setting out along the path, we start the process, we create our own motivation.*

> *Ironically it is often the first step, this beginning, which is the most difficult.'*

> Anthony Grant, *It's Your Life. What are you going to do with it?*

This step is concerned with taking the workable concept or decision and bringing it to life. This stage completes the loop from thought to action. It encourages people to develop nine action steps they can take to bring the decision or workable concept to the marketplace. A wonderful example of this Action stage is the following: 'in the first meeting with a panel of surgeons looking for a new surgical tool, an IDEO employee abruptly left the room. Moments later, he came back with a prototype created from a few office supplies—a marker, a Kodak film canister, and a small orange clip—and handed it to one of the surgeons. The surgeon's response: yeah, I'm thinking of something like this.'[5]

The primary aim of this stage is to transform a concept or potential solution into a tangible action. It could be to develop a prototype, build a business case, conduct some market research or obtain some funding. The emphasis is always on action.

Nine action questions

1. What are we trying to achieve?
2. How will we measure success?
3. Who needs to approve this new project?
4. What resources do we need to make it happen?
5. What is the business case?
6. Can we test the concept quickly, easily and cheaply?
7. Who has responsibility for the various stages of the project?
8. What does a launch plan look like?
9. When will it all happen?

A case study in the Four-step Speed Thinking Cycle: The ten-minute press release

I recently conducted a number of Speed Thinking workshops with a major international public relations firm. As a demonstration of the power of Speed Thinking, we selected the task of writing a press release.

This activity would normally take this group two to three hours, but I suggested we could do it in ten minutes with no drop in quality using a new way of thinking. I used my company as the client and the brief was to write a press release announcing the launch of my new concept, Speed Thinking. The target audience was business leaders generally, but human resource managers in particular.

This is the process we went through:

THE TWO-MINUTE BRIEF

I gave the group two minutes to ask me any question about me, my business, the benefits of Speed Thinking, my client list, and so on.

STEP 1: START—NINE HEADINGS IN TWO MINUTES

Working by themselves, each team member had to write nine possible headlines in two minutes. I suggested to them that they should include a mixture of usual and radical headlines.

STEP 2: EVALUATE THE BEST RATIONAL AND EMOTIONAL HEADLINES

Working with a partner, each pair discussed each other's headlines and agreed on the best rational and emotional headline in a two-minute period.

STEP 3: BUILD STAGE

Each pair then selected their preferred emotional headline and wrote nine key support bullet points under this heading in two minutes.

STEP 4: ACTION STAGE—DEVELOP A WORKABLE DRAFT

Each pair was then given two minutes to convert these bullet points into a workable press release and then we read these out to the rest of the group.

An example of a press release from this process is given below:

'In a world first, Australian thought leader Dr Ken Hudson introduces a brand new way of thinking to organisations across Australia, large and small. He calls this accelerated way of creating ideas, solving problems or making decisions Speed Thinking.

The new approach has been endorsed by major leading global organisations whose productivity has noticeably increased since working with this thinking guru.

This will come as good news for Australian business as we enter a downturn, with clear business benefits, which will come from a faster thinking workforce, being very apparent.'

Summary

In this chapter I have outlined the Four-step Speed Thinking Cycle. I have found that these four steps give a dynamic structure to your intuition. The cycle enables you to start to develop a range of potential solutions, then evaluate an area that you believe is worth exploring further, then try to build a more workable, expanded solution. The last step asks you to take your preferred solution and develop nine ways you can action it.

The emphasis in these four steps is to create movement and momentum. The systematic nature of these four steps ensures that the quality of your result can be surprisingly high, given the short amount of time you have worked on it. In a time-poor world, where performance is everything, the Four-step Speed Thinking Cycle is an ideal way of entering a flow-like state and accelerating quality results day-in, day-out.

PART 2

The practice of Speed Thinking: *Speed Links*

CHAPTER 4

Nine ways to use *Speed Links* to brainstorm ideas

'If I write *rapidly*, putting down my story exactly as it comes into my mind, only looking back to check the names of my characters and the relevant parts of their back stories, I find that I can keep up with my original enthusiasm and at the same time outrun the self-doubt that's always waiting to settle in.'

Stephen King, *On Writing*

Speed Links is the basic Speed Thinking tool. In this chapter I will show you how to use it in many and varied ways. I have used Speed Links in all sorts of situations to create ideas, solve problems or make decisions. *Speed Links* has always helped me or the team that I was working with achieve a breakthrough result. It can be used by an individual or group in a paper-based or electronic format. (There are some blank templates for you to use at the back of the book or visit my website **www.thespeedthinkingzone.com**.)

Nine starting points

The format of *Speed Links* consists of nine large circles, each containing an inner circle. It is deliberately designed so that there is a blank connecting space in the middle of the page. This is your space to connect or link your different initial thoughts. There are nine thought bubbles to mirror the two-minute, nine-possibility Speed Thinking experience. This is different from mind-mapping, for example, where there is a central bubble in the middle of the page. For me, this creates a visual barrier to connecting different thoughts.

The aim of *Speed Links* is to capture your ideas as quickly as you can in a two-minute period without filtering them. You just start. Even with nine starting thoughts, you can theoretically create over 360,000 different combinations (362,880 to be precise).

APPLICATION

A good habit to get into is to write your name, the date and the challenge at the top of the *Speed Links* page. This will make it easier to capture and retrieve the information. (Sometimes I have created a range of wonderful solutions but have forgotten the original problem.)

In two minutes, write down nine initial thoughts in the inner circles. You have begun to start solving the problem or challenge. Select one or more of the inside circles at random, then in the outside circle develop nine ways to make the initial thought stronger.

For example, your initial challenge might be, 'What are nine ways to stop procrastinating?' You might record the following: 'Just start', 'Set a goal', 'Do anything', 'Talk to others who get things done', 'Reward myself when I complete something', 'Do it straight away', 'Punish myself when I procrastinate', 'Imagine I cannot fail', 'Create a radical solution and a usual solution'.

You now have nine potential ways of addressing this challenge. You can select the best one and use the other steps in the Four-step Speed Thinking Cycle (see Chapter 3) to action your selected option.

SPEED LINKS Challenge: ______________________________

Name: ______________________________ Date: ____________

STARTING TIPS

In two minutes, write down nine initial thoughts in the inner circles.

Remember, your brain has a great capacity to 'chunk' or group information, so keep these thoughts as brief as possible. This will ensure that you continue to think quickly without filtering.

It will also mean that you open up, not close down, your initial thoughts.

Expand and connect (nine times)

The second way to use *Speed Links* is to focus on a challenge and create nine possibilities as fast as you can in the inner circles. The next step is to select one or more of these thought bubbles and try to make this initial thought nine times better. You capture these further thoughts on the outside of the inner circle. The advantage of this approach is that you can spend a further two minutes exploring and enhancing your initial ideas before you evaluate these. Select your favourite thought bubble or one at random, and begin.

If you are working with a partner, you can work separately to develop your starting points, then select one or more from each of your *Speed Links* and together build a range of initial thoughts into stronger concepts.

APPLICATION

Let's go back to the challenge in *Speed Links* 1: 'What are nine ways to stop procrastinating?' Some options might include: 'Just start', 'Set a goal', 'Do anything', 'Talk to others who get things done', 'Reward myself when I complete something', 'Do it straight away', 'Punish myself when I procrastinate', 'Imagine I cannot fail', 'Create a radical solution and a usual solution'.

If you select one at random, say 'Reward myself when I complete something', then you would spend two minutes on expanding this thought. For example, 'Have a cup of coffee', 'Go to a movie', 'Exercise', 'Send my list to others for comments', 'Have a night off'.

You could also combine the starting thoughts at random. What might happen if you combine 'Imagine I cannot fail' with 'Do it straight away'? This might lead to 'Consider taking on any challenge immediately', 'Say yes to things that make me feel uncomfortable', 'Go back to university to study', 'Propose to my partner' and so on. The aim is to connect items that normally don't go together and see what happens. In two minutes you might create an original and powerful solution. Perhaps the best way I have found to do this is to number each response (from 1 to 9), then give people two numbers at random (e.g. 3 and 7) and ask them to connect these two initial thoughts.

SPEED LINKS Challenge: ____________________

Name: ____________________ Date: __________

STARTING TIPS

Select one thought bubble and make the initial idea in the inner circle nine times better. Capture your thoughts in the outer circle.

You can also try to connect two of the initial thought bubbles.

Go back to uni

Try to connect these

OR

Connect two bubbles at random

Nine usual and radical ideas

The aim with this variation of *Speed Links* is to create nine usual ideas in two minutes. A usual idea or solution is a continuation of what you have done in the past. You capture these in the inner circles as you move around *Speed Links.*

In the next two minutes, you try to create nine radical ideas around the outside circle. A radical or left-field idea is one that has not been tried before. These radical ideas may or may not be related to the inner, usual ideas.

The benefit of this approach is that each person can create potentially 18 ideas in four minutes. Not only is the quantity high, but you are asking everyone to create two different sets of ideas. By asking people for a range of radical ideas or solutions, you are giving them permission to be innovative and setting a creative expectation.

APPLICATION

This tool can be used by yourself or in a group brainstorming situation. A clever thing to do is to send out the challenge before the session and ask everyone to come along with their nine usual ideas and nine radical ideas completed. In this way, if you invite ten people you can have up to 180 initial ideas as you walk into the room.

Alternatively, you could have half the group develop nine usual ideas and the other half nine radical ideas.

You could also try to connect a number of the radical ideas or a radical idea and a usual idea and see what emerges (see *Speed Links* 2).

SPEED LINKS Challenge: ____________________________

Name: ____________________________ Date: ____________

Radical idea

Usual idea

STARTING TIPS

Capture the usual ideas in the inner circles (in two minutes) and the radical ideas in the outer circles (again, in two minutes).

Then try to connect a few at random and see what emerges.

Nine different lenses

In one of my earlier books, called *The Idea Generator*, I outlined a model of creative thinking which suggested that, if you look at the same problem with the same lens (i.e. perspective), you typically get the same results.[1] To break free of this cycle, you need to either adopt a new lens and/or redefine the challenge.

In this way of using *Speed Links* we will adopt the first strategy. Your aim is simply to list nine different lenses in two minutes. Then you adopt one of these perspectives and new ideas often emerge. When this is done quickly, this strategy seems to work even better. You do not filter your responses, which means that you are more likely to suggest an unusual perspective. The more left-field the lens that you use, the more likely you will create an original idea.

APPLICATION

The aim with this approach is to generate as many different perspectives as possible in two minutes. For example, if you were trying to develop a new product or revenue growth opportunity, you might imagine nine different brands in two minutes (e.g. Sony, Apple, Virgin, Mambo, Ford, Montblanc). Then you would randomly adopt one of these brands' perspectives and see how they would view the marketplace. Adopting Montblanc's view of the world, for example, might lead you to develop a premium version of your product, or a black one, or a more stylish version.

When faced with a new situation, try to identify nine creative people, for example, in two minutes (e.g. Beyoncé, Steve Jobs, Mozart, Jane Campion, Einstein). Then adopt one of their lenses and, in the next two minutes, what new ideas or possibilities might emerge? You might, for example, develop a classical version of your product (based on music by Mozart).

This tool can be used with a partner or group. Have each person write down nine different perspectives on their *Speed Links* and hand this to the next person and ask them to adopt, for example, the number four perspective and start creating ideas. In this way you combine speed, randomness, a different lens and the power of the group—quite a powerful, creative force.

SPEED LINKS Challenge: ______________________________

Name: ______________________________ Date: ____________

Suppliers' attitude

Consumers' attitude

STARTING TIPS

In two minutes, think of nine different perspectives on this issue, challenge or opportunity and write these in the inner circles.

Adopt one or more of these perspectives and create nine new ideas around the outside circle.

Then try to connect another bubble. What new ideas emerge?

Nine emotions

Life is a balance between reason, emotion and imagination. In my PhD thesis I developed a model which suggested that in creative or innovative organisations and teams there needed to be a dynamic tension between these three forces.[2] You might start with an analysis of the market (reason), then a new idea based on a gap in the market (imagination), followed by a dedicated team of innovators to implement this new initiative (emotion).

With this approach the aim is to harness the power and engagement of emotions to create a new idea. Business, law and politics in particular use the language of reason, which makes it hard to access your imagination. Making emotion explicit tends to validate the importance and role of emotions in the creative and decision-making process.

APPLICATION

The aim with this *Speed Links* application is to write down nine different emotions you may feel about a challenge in the next two minutes. For example, if you were trying to reduce the number of customers leaving your business and going to the competition, you might feel the following emotions: sadness, joy (they might be annoying customers), excitement, disloyalty, disappointment, revenge, anger, determination and empathy.

You then select one of these at random (e.g. empathy) and try to develop nine ways you could stem this flow using this emotion. This might lead you to conduct some research with your customers. You might call or email them, asking them to reconsider. They might just want to get something off their chest.

This application can be used by an individual or a group. Each person would create their own set of nine emotions and give it to the other person to work on. The advantage of this approach is that people will normally only focus on emotions that they are comfortable with. Forcing people at random to consider an emotion encourages them to move out of their comfort zone.[3]

SPEED LINKS Challenge: ____________________

Name: ____________________ Date: __________

Joy

Sadness

STARTING TIPS

Think of nine different emotions on this issue, challenge or opportunity in two minutes. Write these in the inner circles.

Then use one or more of these to create nine new ideas in the outer circle.

Or try to connect a number of the thought bubbles and see what new ideas emerge.

Nine pictures

Pictures or images have the advantage that they are often more universal, evocative and emotional than words. From a Speed Thinking point of view, pictures can convey something very quickly. If you are also working with a diverse group where English may be a second language, for example, using pictures or images is a powerful way to communicate.

The aim with this *Speed Links* variation is to try to generate nine different images in two minutes. These can be drawn or selected from a pile of existing images, selected at random. You then select one of these images and in two minutes use this image to create nine new ideas. Repeat this process as often as you wish.

APPLICATION

I have used this approach in many customer service situations. For example, you ask the customer service staff to draw nine images that convey the frustrations that a customer may feel when they deal with your business. Because this must be completed in two minutes, people do not worry about their artistic skills or about being politically correct. They just focus on conveying an idea or feeling.

If you are working with a partner, you might explain each other's drawings then select one frustration to try to address. You then give each pair two minutes to try to reduce or eliminate this frustration. A quick evaluation might follow. For example, 'Which one of these nine suggestions could we introduce next week?' The final stage might see you designing nine action steps to introduce this course of action. You have now completed a Four-step Speed Thinking Cycle in less than ten minutes and have potentially reduced or eliminated a customer frustration. Your customers will love you for it.

This approach is also fun to do on a large whiteboard with a group. You have each person stand before the whiteboard and draw their images. An amazing creative energy is created quickly when everyone is drawing together. You can then compare and connect your different drawings, which might just unlock an original idea.

SPEED LINKS Challenge: ______________________________

Name: ______________________________ Date: ____________

STARTING TIPS

In two minutes, draw nine different images in the inner circles relating to a specific challenge.

If you have a collection of existing images, ask everyone to select nine images in two minutes.

Then use one or more of these drawings or images to create nine new ideas in the outer circle in two minutes.

Nine headlines

Have you ever smiled at a good headline in a newspaper or magazine? From a Speed Thinking point of view, in just a few words the writer has been able to convey the essence of a story—its colour and movement—and invoke a response. Who said that you needed large volumes of information to convey something? To borrow from Shakespeare, 'brevity is the soul of wit'.

In this application of *Speed Links*, people are asked to write nine short headlines about a challenge in two minutes. I have found that the sharpness and discipline of writing headlines require creativity, but the time and challenge requirement forces people not to filter their ideas and encourages humorous and clever work.

APPLICATION

This approach can be used by an individual, in pairs or in a group. You are given a challenge and in the next two minutes you write as many different headlines (or single key words) as you can in the inner circles. Then you might explain your initial ideas to a partner, who can do the same (in two minutes). Then try to combine one of your headlines with one of your partner's headlines and see what happens.

Select a headline at random, or the most emotional, then create nine new ideas. For example, if I was trying to think of ideas to promote Speed Thinking, I might come up with the headline 'Faster than Andy Roddick' (he has the fastest serve in men's tennis). This might lead me to hold a promotion on a tennis court, create an idea faster than a tennis player could serve, have Andy Roddick promote Speed Thinking, conduct a session at a race track, serve people nine jelly beans on a plate to emphasise the number, sponsor a speed cooking television program, and so on.

SPEED LINKS Challenge: ____________________

Name: ____________________ Date: __________

How to speed legally

Faster than your computer!

STARTING TIPS

In two minutes, write in the inner circles nine different headlines (or key words) relating to a challenge.

Then select one or more of these at random and use the headline to create nine new ideas in the outer circle in two minutes.

Nine scenes

Have you ever enjoyed a good movie and discussed your favourite scene with your friends? From a Speed Thinking point of view, every movie is just a collection of individual but coherent scenes. Each scene has a purpose and must contribute to the overall narrative that the director is trying to convey.

With this approach you ask a group of people to construct a story about a particular issue in two minutes, with each person describing one scene.

The advantage of this *Speed Links* application is that it encourages participants to work together in a playful and constructive way, to stay in the moment and to readily accept the ideas of others. One person starts by describing a scene and then the other person must quickly follow their lead by describing another scene. This is similar to the concept in improvisation of acceptance or 'yes and' whereby you must readily accept whatever is offered by another person.[4]

At the end of this exercise, people are often amazed at the twists and turns that unfold and the ideas and insights that emerge.

APPLICATION

This *Speed Links* application is an ideal one to use in a group. With a group of nine, each person can contribute a single scene. With a smaller group, participants can each contribute a number of scenes.

The group is given a challenge and in two minutes they must construct a series of nine scenes without talking to one another. This forces people to draw (right-brain activity) and interpret the previous scene. The group must then create nine new ideas from one scene or nine insights to the challenge that emerged from the exercise after discussing the new story that has developed from the nine scenes.

SPEED LINKS Challenge: ____________________

Name: ____________________ Date: __________

Person singing

In the field

STARTING TIPS

If you are working in a group, ask each person to draw one scene in the inner circle that builds on the previous one. All the scenes should be completed in two minutes.

An amazing story will often emerge. Then concentrate on the entire narrative or a specific scene. What are nine insights or ideas that might emerge?

Catch a ball (nine times)

The essence of Speed Thinking is that, because you are working so quickly, you have no time to filter or self-censor your thoughts, goals, plans or dreams, nor are you restricted by the expectations of others. This is sometimes easier said than done.

I have found that a good way to overcome your often nagging internal critical voice is to distract it by catching a ball.[5] By concentrating on catching a ball, participants allow their unconscious mind to wander and, as a result, often come up with powerful new ideas. 'Where did that come from?' is an often-heard comment from participants when they use this activity.

APPLICATION

This way of using *Speed Links* is ideal for a group of three or more. One person throws the ball, the other catches it and the third person captures the thoughts of the other two.

Each group of three is given a challenge and asked to come up with nine new ideas in two minutes. One person starts and throws the ball to the other. They must catch the ball and build on their thought and return the ball in an instant. This back and forth goes on for two minutes and/or until they have created nine new thoughts.

This exercise is fun and the ball feels like a 'hot potato' that people want to get rid of as soon as possible, which encourages them not to filter their ideas. The other benefit is that it combines the physical with the mental and the subsequent creative energy is immense.

SPEED LINKS Challenge: ______________________________

Name: ______________________________ Date: ____________

Teenage version

iPhone application

STARTING TIPS

Work in groups of three. As one person throws the ball to a partner, they must offer a new thought, which the third person then writes in the inner circle.

The second person must then build on that idea. Try to go back and forth nine times in two minutes.

Then select one or more thought bubbles and repeat the exercise using the initial idea as a starting point.

Final note

How you use *Speed Links* to brainstorm ideas depends on you. I have outlined nine possible uses that have worked for me over the years and these all work. You can create a new set of applications that build on the visual and connective nature of the *Speed Links* design.

There is no right or wrong approach. It will depend on your preference, the situation and whether you are using it in a group situation. By following these suggestions you will gain more confidence in your ability to think of big, new ideas in minutes. These *Speed Links* options can be used with great effect in combination. With these different formats you will never 'get stuck' and you will be armed for your next meeting with plenty of new ideas. Remember, this is the start of the process, not the end. The ideas that you have created are now ready to be developed by using the Four-step Speed Thinking Cycle.

‘Research has repeatedly shown that timely decisions based on less information frequently generate equal or better results than delayed but more fully analysed decision making.’

Christopher Witt, Director of the Centre for Innovation and Entrepreneurship, Australian School of Business

CHAPTER 5

Nine ways to use *Speed Links* to make better, faster decisions (and stop procrastinating)

'The reality is that the classical model of decision making doesn't work very well in practice. It works tolerably well in the research labs which use undergraduate test subjects making trivial decisions, but it doesn't do so well in the real world, where decisions are more challenging, situations are more confusing and complex, information is scarce or inconclusive, time is short and stakes are high.'

Gary Klein, *The Power of Intuition*

Nine pros and cons

The primary aim of this set of decision-making *Speed Links* applications is to show you that there can be a middle ground with decision-making for everyday decisions.

Those in the traditional camp of decision-making place emphasis on considering a range of options, carefully weighing each up and making a rational, objective decision. However, by using our left brain we tend to only consider a few incremental options and the impact of each one is not known in advance.

There are others who suggest that people should only rely on their intuition or gut feelings. For people who have experience in a particular field, this is a very effective and incredibly quick way to make decisions.[1] However, intuition relies on extensive experience, is an internal process and is difficult to teach.

There is a third way, which is faster than traditional decision-making yet provides intuition with greater rigour, structure and openness. It is called Speed Decision-making and it is ideal for a fast-paced world in which we have to constantly make everyday decisions.[2]

The first application of *Speed Links* for decision-making is an old favourite with a twist. With this use you simply list nine pros of a potential decision in the inner circles and nine cons in the surrounding circles in two minutes each. By doing so you will greatly expand the number of factors to consider (most people only consider two to four) and by doing this quickly you will not filter your responses.

APPLICATION

This application can be used by an individual or in a group. Your aim is to try to create as many different pros and cons as you can think of in two minutes. This might unlock new angles on a decision that you might not have considered.

If you are working with a group, you could have half the group developing pros and the other half cons. Then compare and contrast your list using your *Speed Links.* Alternatively, you could have the group do all the pros, discuss these and then capture the cons, discuss and agree on the most salient considerations.

After developing the pros and cons list, you will be better placed to make a good decision in minutes. The following applications of *Speed Links* will give you more confidence and with practice you can increase your decision-making success rate.

SPEED LINKS Challenge: ______________________________

Name: ______________________________ Date: ____________

Con

Pro

Con

Pro

STARTING TIPS

Write your pros in the inner circles and the cons in the outer circles (two minutes for each).

You could then compare each pro and con in each thought bubble and, if the pro felt stronger, you could give it a plus 1. If the con felt stronger, it might score a minus 1. (If both are the same, then it is a zero.)

Then add up your scores and you have your decision.

Nine head and heart

This application of *Speed Links* is similar to the first, but uses a different language. We are increasingly realising that emotions (what I have called 'heart') are an integral part of decision-making. In fact, research with patients who have damaged the emotional part of their brain suggests that these people seem almost incapable of making up their mind. As renowned psychologist Antonio Damasio observes, 'at their best, feelings point us in the proper direction, take us to the appropriate place in a decision-making space, where we may put the instruments of logic to good use'.[3]

I designed this variation for business people because the language of business is cold and impersonal and I found that when managers were making decisions they tended to consider only the rational factors, or they talked only about these elements as being important.

This approach encourages leaders to make the rational factors (e.g. cost) and emotional factors (e.g. risk) explicit and equally valid.

APPLICATION

In the first two minutes, write down nine 'heart' (emotional) factors of a decision in the inner circles. In the next two minutes, capture all the 'head' factors in the outer circles. Then you can discuss, compare and contrast all these factors and make a better decision.

I used this application of *Speed Links* when I was talking to a group of television station leaders who were considering moving offices from a trendy suburb to an inner-city one. They (mostly men) highlighted to me all the rational advantages of moving (e.g. lower rent, greater floor space, proximity to public transport). I then asked if there were any emotional factors. Spontaneously, many of the female leaders wrote the word 'safety'. They explained that they did not feel safe in this new location and would not take that risk and were likely to resign. They were convinced that many other female managers and staff members would feel the same. This led to a major rethink of the decision. The move was cancelled and the decision was taken to go back to the existing landlord and try to negotiate a cheaper lease.

By capturing the rational and emotional factors quickly, you do not filter these, and the 'heart' elements are treated as equally valid. In addition, by making the emotional factors explicit, these can be brought out into the open for all to discuss.

SPEED LINKS Challenge: ____________________

Name: ____________________ Date: __________

Learn new skills

Impact on my friends

More pay

What if I fail?

STARTING TIPS

Write your 'heart' considerations in the inner circles in two minutes and the 'head' considerations in the outer circles (again, in two minutes).

In four minutes you have identified eighteen potential factors in a decision, all of varying importance. Making these explicit means that you can discuss these with others and reach a better decision.

Nine stakeholders

This *Speed Links* approach pushes decision-makers to consider a wide variety of inputs. One of the biggest criticisms of leaders' decisions is that they only consider the impact a decision may have on a few stakeholders. Not surprisingly, there is a reluctance to agree with these decisions and possibly puzzlement (why didn't they ask us?). Because it is not possible to talk to everyone in advance, I designed the nine stakeholders application.

Some people have asked me why the stakeholders can't just be listed on a lined A4 page. My reply is that I like visual tools and I believe these can help the decision-making process. The *Speed Links* design has a wonderful, open, connecting space in the middle. Participants in my workshops often comment that this design is appealing, easy, simple, different, thought-provoking and encourages a higher number of possibilities than a more linear approach.

Speed Links not only makes it easier to connect different ideas, perspectives or thoughts, but it also encourages you to make decisions using both the right and left parts of your brain. As Jonah Lehrer notes, 'The simple truth of the matter is that making good decisions requires us to use both sides of the mind. For too long, we've treated human nature as an either/or situation. We are either rational or irrational. We either rely on statistics or trust our gut instincts. Not only are these dichotomies false, they're destructive.'[4]

APPLICATION

When you are faced with a decision, try to list all the possible stakeholders that might be affected by the decision in two minutes. For example, if you were a parent considering taking up a new job offer in another city, you might list yourself, your partner, your kids, your parents, your partner's parents, and so on.

Capture these various stakeholders in the inner circles, then adopt one of these perspectives and consider this decision from their point of view, recording your ideas in the outer circles. Then move on to another perspective and repeat the process. After three or four iterations, you will be in a much better position to make a decision. If you are working with a group, you might have everyone in the group adopt a different viewpoint and discuss your potential decision.

SPEED LINKS Challenge: ______________________________

Name: ______________________________ Date: ______________

Ease of access

Customers

STARTING TIPS

In two minutes, capture in the inner circles nine people that might be affected by a decision.

Then adopt a few of their perspectives and in two minutes record in the outer circles how they might be affected.

Travelling time

Employees

Nine people I admire

Have you ever faced a decision and wondered what another person might do? You sometimes come across this situation in golf when your playing partner or opponent is facing a difficult shot. The golf coaches suggest that to improve your mental game you imagine yourself as that player and think about what sort of shot you might play.

In this application of *Speed Links*, you try to imagine what the decision might be if it were taken by someone you admire. By thinking about nine different perspectives of people you admire, you will increase your chances of making a better decision.

APPLICATION

In two minutes, write down the names of nine people you admire in the inner circles. Don't filter. It could be someone famous or your old schoolteacher. They might be living or dead. Make the list as diverse as possible.

Now choose one of these people and consider the pending decision from their perspective in the next two minutes. Ask yourself what they would do in these circumstances and why. For example, let's imagine you were thinking of changing your child's school and you might admire the way Roger Federer carries himself on a tennis court. Now this great tennis player and your decision about your child's school are unlikely bedfellows, but adopting the Swiss master's mindset you might ask yourself, 'Does the new school have a language program?' (Federer can speak four languages), 'Does the new school have a calm feel to it?' and so on.

With this application, you should regularly vary the people that you admire and select a person at random. If you are working in a group, each person might adopt their fourth favourite person (after you have numbered all nine) and make a decision based on their perspective. The group decision might just help you make a better individual decision.

SPEED LINKS Challenge: ____________________

Name: ____________________ Date: __________

Why?

My daughter

STARTING TIPS

In two minutes, write in the inner circles the names of nine people you admire. The more diverse the better.

Then adopt a few of their perspectives and in two minutes write in the the outer circle what decision they might make and why.

Is it fair?

Martin Luther King

Nine possible decisions

Implicit in the previous few applications of *Speed Links* is the idea that you are having difficulty making a decision about a range of different options. But what if you do not have a range of choices in the first place?

The emphasis here is to generate nine potential decision options in two minutes and then select a few at random and explore what might happen.

One of the major problems of decision-making is that you only have a few options to consider and that many options are so similar there are very few real possibilities. This tool tries to rectify this by helping you generate a greater range of potential decisions and a large diversity between them.

APPLICATION

Let's imagine you are frustrated at your work. Potential decisions you could make might include leaving, looking for a new job, enrolling in some further study, talking to your boss, considering an entirely new career, travelling for a few weeks, starting yoga, taking on a new role in your current job or talking to your partner regularly. All of these decision options might be worth exploring further.

Record the decision options in the inner circles on the *Speed Links* in two minutes. Select a few at random and conduct a pros and cons comparison on each one (in two minutes each). This will force you to consider a decision possibility that you might initially ignore.

If you are working in a group, you might first generate nine decision possibilities and then ask each group member to forcefully argue that this decision is the best one on offer.

To create more variety in your decision possibilities you might also develop, say, five usual decision options and four radical ones (e.g. 'Why don't I travel for a year around the world?) By doing so, you explore more decision options and you are faced with a real decision among quite different alternatives.

SPEED LINKS Challenge: ______________________________

Name: ______________________________ Date: ______________

Pros vs Cons

Do nothing

STARTING TIPS

In two minutes, write down nine possible decisions in the inner circles.

Select one possibility at random and conduct a pros and cons comparison in the next two minutes. Repeat for a range of options.

Then try connecting two thought bubbles at random and create a new possibility.

Pros vs Cons

Talk to my boss

Nine things that could go wrong

One of the biggest barriers to effective decision-making is a constant worry about what might go wrong. This state of mind often means that people are too fearful to make a decision. This can lead to chronic procrastination and lack of confidence. It is also an unproductive use of your emotional energy because people in these situations spend too much time worrying about consequences that might not happen or over which they have no control.

This application of *Speed Links* is designed to overcome this barrier. It encourages you to list what could go wrong and what you could do about it. I have found in my Speed Thinking workshops that having participants highlight what could go wrong in a safe, energising environment often enables them to take more risks. Sometimes just writing a fear down can make it easier to deal with.

APPLICATION

In two minutes, write in the inner circles as many different things as you can think of that could go wrong in selecting a particular decision option. For example, in deciding to sell your house, things that might go wrong could include: you receive no bids, the bids are not high enough, buyers drop out at the last moment, the real estate agent is lazy, you have to keep your house clean, and so on. In two minutes for each one, record in the outer circles nine ways to overcome each of the things that might go wrong. If you can do this, you have nothing to fear.

If you are working with a partner or group, you might have others work on another decision alternative in a similar manner and then compare and contrast your responses. You will then be able to make a better decision by not being paralysed by what might go wrong.

SPEED LINKS Challenge: ______________________________

Name: ______________________________ Date: ____________

But I could make money

I could lose money

I have learned something new

What if it fails?

STARTING TIPS

In two minutes, write in the inner circles nine things that could go wrong with a particular decision.

Select one at random and write in the outer circle nine possible ways that consequence might be avoided or overcome.

Repeat this process for a few other consequences and then make a decision.

Nine decisions today

I believe that good decision-making is a skill that everyone can learn with the right tools and plenty of practice. It is no surprise that people who run successful small businesses or rise up the corporate ladder often do so because they are not scared of making timely decisions. As former CEO of General Electric Jack Welch observes, 'when I asked myself, how many times should I have held off on a decision versus how many times do I wish I'd made that move faster, I inevitably found that the latter won almost every time'.[5]

The thought behind this use of *Speed Links* is to encourage you to actually make decisions. Decision-making begets decisions. Before you know it, the small decisions will transform into big decisions.

APPLICATION

In two minutes, write in the inner circle nine decisions you can make today. These may be tiny and inconsequential, but decisions that should be made nevertheless. These might include what way to drive to work, what to eat for lunch, who to have a morning coffee with, which customer to call, and so on.

The aim is to list all the decisions you have to make and tick these off when you have made a decision. If you get stuck, focus on this decision and do a two-minute pros and cons (or any of the other tools described in this chapter) and then make a decision.

The emphasis with this tool is to make nine decisions today. It is not to worry about the success or otherwise of the decisions. Not making a decision in a fast-paced world, I believe, is the kiss of death. As Virgin founder Richard Branson suggests, 'I have always made fast decisions and acted on my instinct'.[6] The aim, to use a basketball analogy, is to keep shooting for baskets and the ball will eventually go in. If you do not shoot, you will never score.

In my Speed Thinking workshops this is a common issue. People seem genuinely scared of making a decision and the longer they wait the worse it becomes for them. This *Speed Links* application will get you back into the habit of making decisions.

SPEED LINKS Challenge: ______________________________

Name: ______________________________ Date: ____________

The old car needs repairing

Should I have my car serviced?

STARTING TIPS

In two minutes, write in the inner circles nine decisions that you can make today.

If you get stuck on a particular decision, write down nine pros and cons of this decision in the outer circle. If it makes sense, do it!

I do not have the time

Should I have a hair cut?

Nine procrastination-busting questions

One of the insights I have gained from people who procrastinate is that they are aware of their problem, understand the negative consequences and genuinely want to do something about it. Just as decision-making is a habit, so too is procrastination. But why do we procrastinate? According to research, there are three main reasons:

- fear of failure
- fear of making a mistake
- fear of success.[7]

This *Speed Links* approach aims to help you break free of the procrastination habit.

APPLICATION

When you are faced with a decision and you find yourself procrastinating, spend two minutes writing down nine procrastination-busting questions in the inner circles. For example, 'Why am I delaying?', 'Why not start now?', 'What's stopping me?', 'Am I worried about anything with this decision?', 'If so, what?'

Select one of these questions at random and answer it in two minutes. Try to develop nine ways of addressing this question in the outer circle. Repeat this process until you feel more confident in making a decision.

I have found that by making your procrastination-busting questions more tangible and explicit you can develop specific ways of addressing these, which increases your chances of making a decision.

If you know someone else who has a tendency to delay, you can complete your *Speed Links* by yourself then compare notes and inspire each other to make a decision. Remember, the emphasis is on making a decision, not whether it is right or wrong.

SPEED LINKS Challenge: ____________________

Name: ____________________ Date: __________

Nothing!

What's stopping me?

It might not work out but so what?

What am I really risking?

STARTING TIPS

Every time you are faced with a day-to-day decision and you find yourself putting it off, spend two minutes writing down nine procrastination-busting questions in the inner circles.

Select one question at random and answer it in two minutes. Repeat the process until you feel more confident in making a decision.

Connect two of the circles. Is there a way you can address both of these barriers?

Nine unconscious factors

Research by A Dijksterhuis and his team suggests that people using a conscious process make better decisions when they have to select between simple products (e.g. purchasing a toaster).[8] By contrast, people relying on more unconscious processes make better choices among complex products with many variables (e.g. purchasing an apartment). They believe this is due to the following factors:

- The unconscious has a greater capacity to handle more information.
- Conscious thought is limited by expectancies and schemas.
- The unconscious is more able to weigh the relative importance of various attributes.
- Unconscious thought is more divergent.

This fascinating research suggests that the unconscious may have a very active role in decision-making, creative thinking and problem-solving. This *Speed Links* application attempts to provide structure to the unconscious process.

APPLICATION

When you are faced with a relatively complex (but not life-changing) decision, try using your unconscious to make a decision. In two minutes, write in the inner circles the first nine thoughts on this subject that pop into your mind, without filtering. For example, we are debating whether to buy a new car for my wife. The first nine things that jump into my mind are 'image', 'fun', 'colour', 'smile', 'pride', 'cost', 'deserving', 'daughter' and 'sign'. Place each of these in the centre of the inner circle. Select one at random (e.g. pride) and allow your unconscious to ruminate again for two minutes. For example, 'Why pride?', 'Brand new', 'My wife has never had a new car', 'What brand would she be most proud of?', 'Do we need a brand?', 'My kids might be proud'. Capture these thoughts in the outer circle.

These sorts of emerging thoughts might help you to better access your unconscious, understand what is happening and help you make a better decision. The important point with this tool is not to filter or analyse, but simply to let your unconscious flow.

SPEED LINKS Challenge: ______________________________

Name: ______________________________ Date: ____________

Sign

STARTING TIPS

When faced with a complex decision, take two minutes to write down the first nine things that come into your head in the inner circles.

Select one of these and try to capture nine other thoughts in the outer circle.

After a few minutes, you have a better understanding of your unconscious decision-making process, which should help you make a better decision.

Daughter

CHAPTER 6

Nine ways to use *Speed Links* to solve a problem

'The best way to overcome your fear of creativity, brainstorming, intelligent risk taking or navigating a tricky situation might be to sprint.

When we sprint, all the internal dialogue falls away and we just go as fast as we possibly can. When you're sprinting you don't feel that sore knee and you don't worry that the ground isn't perfectly level. You just run.

You can't sprint forever. That's what makes it sprinting. The brevity of the event is a key part of why it works.'

Seth Godin blog, author of *Permission Marketing* and *Unleash the Idea Virus*

Nine solutions in two minutes

Have you ever felt stuck in a day-to-day problem in which you go round in circles or you avoid it altogether?

With this application of *Speed Links*, you put two minutes aside to focus on the problem at hand. For many everyday problems you already have a rich array of possible solutions or experiences to call on. You simply need a way of enabling these to emerge. My experience is that asking people to create nine solutions in two minutes forces them to focus and numerous initial solutions or starting points arise. As intuition expert Gary Klein observes, 'when we are faced with a familiar problem, there is a good chance that the first solution we recognise is going to work'.[1]

Also, by using the *Speed Links* visual design with its distinctive circles and with the emphasis on expanding and connecting possibilities, you can use more of your right brain to solve problems. As psychology professors John Kounios and Mark Jung-Beeman discovered, people who solve problems methodically have different brain activity than people who solve problems using a creative insight. One difference is that creative problem-solvers exhibit greater activity in several regions of the right hemisphere.[2]

APPLICATION

In two minutes, write in the inner circles nine potential solutions to the problem. For example, how could you encourage drivers to slow down in your street? You could turn it into a cul-de-sac, place signs asking drivers to slow down, show pictures of kids, talk to drivers when they stop, place an open letter in the local neighborhood newspaper or letterboxes, and so on.

Try to randomly connect a number of the inner circles to build a better solution. Alternatively, focus on one initial thought and, in the outer circle, make this initial thought nine times better.

If you are working in a group, have each person write down their first nine solutions then swap their *Speed Links* and ask the other person to enhance or connect some of the inner circles.

SPEED LINKS Challenge: ____________________

Name: ____________________ Date: __________

Make this nine times better

Initial solution 1

Initial solution 2

STARTING TIPS

Clear your mind of everything for the next few minutes.

Write the problem down at the top of this page. In two minutes, write in the inner circles the first nine solutions that come into your head. Remember not to filter your thoughts.

Select a few solutions at random, then try to make these nine times better or try to connect a few and explore what happens.

Nine new questions

To solve a problem in an original way, we have to ask new questions. As Einstein said, 'we can't solve problems by using the same kind of thinking we used when we created them'. The aim of this variation of *Speed Links* is to develop nine new questions about a problem.[3]

A new question is one to which you genuinely do not know the answer. It should stop and make you think. Sometimes it is a completely naive question that you have long since dismissed. This is why it is good idea when you are forming a new group to have people who are close to the problem and others who are outside of it. These people will ask the obvious, simple questions which might just unlock a new solution.

APPLICATION

In the inner circles, write down as many new questions as you can think of in two minutes. For example, if the problem was to obtain a better work/life balance, new questions might include 'What would I do with the extra time?', 'Could I still pay all my bills?', 'What might my friends think?', 'What might my boss say?', 'Who could I share the extra time with?'

Any of these new questions then becomes the springboard for a potential new set of solutions. Select one or more of these questions and try to develop nine new answers. For example, if you selected 'What would I do with the extra time?', you might answer: 'Study', 'Play sport', 'Take up yoga', 'Read more', 'Walk on the beach', 'Become involved in a charity or cause'.

If you are working in a group or with a partner, try to develop nine new questions then swap your *Speed Links* with your partner and address some or all of your partner's questions. Alternatively, select the most original question and both of you solve it, then compare answers.

The aim with this use of *Speed Links* is to try to create a new question. By doing so, you are halfway to designing a fresh solution.

SPEED LINKS Challenge: ______________________________

Name: ______________________________ Date: ____________

Could we develop a kids' version?

STARTING TIPS

Develop nine new questions in two minutes and write these in the inner circles.

Now select one or more at random and try to develop nine potential answers to this question in two minutes. Record your answers in the outer circle.

What about a simpler version?

Nine ways to define the problem

We have been taught that there is always one correct way to define a problem. The challenge seems to be to find exactly what that is. This is classic cause-and-effect linear thinking. However, most problems have multiple causes that are connected. In this type of traditional thinking, the emphasis often is on trying to define the problem in the correct way rather than actually trying to solve it.

To design original solutions, this application of *Speed Links* encourages you to explore new ways of defining the problem. I have been involved in many workshops where participants have expended enormous energy arguing about why their definition of a problem was the correct and only one. They spent so much time trying to agree on what the problem was, that very little time was spent designing solutions.

APPLICATION

Create nine different problem definitions in two minutes and write them in the inner circles. Select one or more of these and try to develop nine possible solutions in two minutes. Write the solutions in the outer circle.

For example, let's imagine that sales were below budget. This may be due to a sales forecasting problem or a sales skill problem or an advertising budget problem. All of these problems are interrelated and may not be any more correct than the others, but the solution may involve all of these.

If you are working with a group or partner, you each define the problem in as many ways as you can without filtering in two minutes. Then discuss the definitions and select the most original ones or the ones that make you feel uncomfortable or one selected at random.

The emphasis with this use of *Speed Links* is to shift your thinking from one of striving to have the correct problem definition to having a range of workable solutions. The problem definition is the means to the end, not an end in itself.

SPEED LINKS Challenge: ____________________

Name: ____________________ Date: __________

Benchmark

Product quality problem

STARTING TIPS

Develop nine different ways of defining the problem in two minutes and write these in the inner circles. Now try to combine two bubbles and see what happens.

Select one or more at random and try to develop nine potential solutions in another two minutes. Write the solutions in the outer circle.

Skill problem

Nine emotional ways to define the problem

This application of *Speed Links* builds on the previous one. The language of business, politics and law is rational. Think of cost-cutting, efficiency, downsizing, structure, and so on. This often means that the way you define a problem is also in cold, faceless terms. For example, 'How can we improve our customer satisfaction levels by 10 per cent?' This emphasis on being objective might work well in the analytical stage but it does not generate alternative ways to define the problem. Rational problem definitions often trap people into rational, incremental solutions.

Emotions are the pathway to the imagination. If you define a problem that excites and engages yourself and others, you will be more interested in solving it and more creative in your solutions.[4]

APPLICATION

With this application of *Speed Links*, your aim is to generate nine emotional problem definitions as quickly as you can. For example, let's imagine that the problem is an employee who is constantly late for work. This puts pressure on the rest of the team and can affect workloads and perhaps customer service. Using this application you would aim to create nine emotional problem definitions (hint: the shorter the better). These might include: the problem is a lack of motivation, passion, unfairness to other staff, stress it causes you, broken promise, disappointment, wasted potential, enjoyment, and so on.

Now suddenly I feel that there is an expanded range of related problem definitions where the solution can emerge. For example, if you take one area—the problem is that the employee's lateness causes you stress—you could then try to develop nine potential solutions: dismiss the employee, talk to the employee about the stress it causes you, enrol in a yoga class, pass this stress back to the employee, and so on.

If you are working in a group, one person can use *Speed Links* to develop nine emotional ways of defining a problem then pass it on to another, who must select one at random and try to solve it. After a few turns (all in two minutes), the group comes back together and discusses the various options and decides what is the best course of action.

SPEED LINKS Challenge: ______________________________

Name: ______________________________ Date: ____________

Lock them out if they arrive late

I hate people being late for meetings

STARTING TIPS

Develop nine emotional ways of defining the problem in two minutes and write these in the inner circles.

Select a number of these and try to solve the problem in another two minutes. Write the solutions in the outer circles.

Nine solution barriers

The aim of this application of *Speed Links* is to turn our attention to the solution space that is available to us. This is an often ignored aspect of any problem-solving process. The smaller the solution space, the smaller the options. A large field means you can play various sports or activities, for example, soccer, hockey, cricket, rugby etc. If, however, the space is ten metres by ten metres, the range of options is decreased significantly.

This application of *Speed Links* encourages you to think more creatively about the solution space you have available and how you can expand it. Remember, the solution barriers can be tangible (e.g. budget) or intangible (e.g. attitude to risk, openness to new ideas).

APPLICATION

In two minutes, capture nine solution barriers in the inner circles. For example, the challenge may be how to launch a new product. Some of the solution barriers might be: budget, PR support, brand positioning, competition, relationships with retailers, consumer profile.

Then select one or more of these in order of importance or at random. If you selected PR support, for example, ways you could expand your solution space might be to contact small PR companies, blog young PR graduates, phone writers in the press, email websites, ask friends for some recommendations, and so on.

If you are working in a group, have each group develop nine solution barriers in two minutes, then swap the *Speed Links*, select a few at random and create ways to expand the space. Then discuss your ideas and agree upon an action plan to make this a reality.

The aim with this process is to expand the space that you have available. By doing so, you can expand the number and range of solution possibilities.

SPEED LINKS Challenge: ______________________________

Name: ______________________________ Date: ______________

Form a partnership

Money

STARTING TIPS

Capture nine solution barriers in two minutes (e.g. money, time, people, technology) and write these in the inner circles.

You could create nine tangible barriers, then nine intangible ones (e.g. openness to new ideas).

Select a number of these and in two minutes try to write nine ways you can expand this solution space. Then try to connect a few of these and see what emerges.

Nine parts to the problem

Most big problems have many different parts and you can decide to concentrate on the entire problem or select a component of the problem that you wish to focus on. For example, if the problem is 'I am always running late for meetings', some of the areas that you could focus on might include your schedule, the hours you are working, your workload, your job description, the meeting length or location. Any of these factors or a combination of them could provide the key to unlocking a new solution.

This application of *Speed Links* forces you to consider at least nine different parts of any problem. By trying to solve one part of this puzzle, you are closer to developing a total solution. Remember, you can decide which part of the problem you wish to start working on, and in what detail.

APPLICATION

In two minutes, write in the inner circles all the potential parts to the problem. You are not seeking solutions at this stage but just to highlight the potential areas of interest. For example, if you are talking about trying to fix traffic congestion in the city, you could concentrate on the number of cars, the traffic light system, police directions, time of the day, road design, driver education, public transport alternatives, and so on. As you can see, most big problems have multiple and overlapping factors to consider. Try to record these in your *Speed Links* quickly so that you do not filter any issue.

After capturing these factors, select one or more and try to develop nine ways of resolving this part of the problem in two minutes. You can then evaluate these alternatives, develop a better solution and create an action plan to test some of these solutions (following the Four-step Speed Thinking Cycle outlined in Chapter 3).

If you are working in a group, ask each group member to focus on one part of the problem and present their suggestions to the group. Then look for potential overlaps or common solutions.

SPEED LINKS Challenge: ______________________

Name: ______________________ Date: __________

Expand the peak period

Timing

STARTING TIPS

Capture nine parts to the problem (e.g. people, skills, timing) in two minutes and write these in the inner circles.

Select a number of these and try to write nine ways you could solve this part of the problem. Then try to connect a few of these solutions and see what emerges.

Nine features of the ideal solution

If you were trying to design a computer for kids, where would you start? Most people would suggest making the buttons bigger, or adding more colour or having kids' software built in. There is nothing wrong with this approach—it is sound, practical and makes perfect sense. However, if you are trying to come up with an original solution, this may not be the way to go.

Starting with what exists and moving forward forces you to think in an incremental way. What if your starting point is 'what does the ideal computer for kids look like'? From this blank page anything is possible. Perhaps it is something that could be rolled from room to room, that you could sit on or climb inside? With an ideal computer in mind, you can design back to where you are today.

APPLICATION

This application of *Speed Links* challenges you to design nine features of the ideal solution as quickly as you can. With this approach, speed is of the essence—you do not want your internal critical voice telling you all the things that you cannot do or that are not practical or seem silly. (Who would have thought a few years ago that the world's most innovative product would be a phone or that kids today would not wear watches?)

Record nine aspects of the ideal solution in two minutes in the inner circles. Then select all or some of these features and work out how you can make each feature come alive. In the above example, think of the feature that allows the kids' computer to roll from room to room. This might lead you to a computer on wheels, a ball-shaped computer, an extra-light PC, it might be part of a walking-type frame, and so on.

You then might connect these inner circle solutions with others across *Speed Links* at random, trying to build a bigger, better solution. Then use the Four-step Speed Thinking Cycle to help you filter or sort out the most promising ideas.

If you are working in a larger group, one small group could take each feature of the ideal solution (e.g. it must be scratch-proof) and play around with this and find a way for it to work.

SPEED LINKS Challenge: ______________________________

Name: ______________________________ Date: ____________

Research with kids

Fun to use

STARTING TIPS

Think of nine features of the ideal solution in two minutes and write these in the inner circles.

Select a number of these features and in the outer circles write down nine ways you can bring each feature to life. Look to combine and connect these in unusual ways.

Then use the Four-step Speed Thinking Cycle to build a better solution.

Nine uncomfortable solutions

When I am working with a group to solve a difficult problem, I often challenge them to create a range of solutions that make them feel uncomfortable. My reason for doing this is that most of us like to work within our comfort zone. Managers, in particular, say they want to be challenged but in reality often mean only within their comfort zone.

This application of *Speed Links* encourages you to create and explore those uncomfortable potential solutions. In my experience, most of the truly original solutions that people have developed often started with a feeling of discomfort. I have also found that the more you work these solutions, the less scary they seem. Often at the end of a session, people wonder what the initial fuss was about.

Moving people out of their comfort zone also might give you an edge on your competition if they stay within their current paradigm or existing 'rules of the game'.

APPLICATION

Decide on your challenge, then try to develop nine potential solutions that make you feel uncomfortable and write these in the inner circles. Again, try to do this as quickly as you can so you do not filter your responses. You do not have to justify or explain to anyone why a particular solution makes you feel this way. At this stage you are relying on your personal intuition. This is a desirable thing to do, as this will vary from person to person—your uncomfortable solution might not go far enough for others.

Now select one or more of these uncomfortable solutions and, in the outer circles, try to develop nine ways of making these simpler or more acceptable or practical. If you are working in a group, each person could take one of these uncomfortable raw solutions and try to make it less threatening.

After you have completed this stage, discuss your suggestions with your colleagues or a partner and, if you both see merit, move to the other steps in the Four-step Speed Thinking Cycle (i.e. Evaluate, Build, Action).

SPEED LINKS Challenge: ______________________________

Name: ______________________________ Date: ____________

Offer a smaller prize

Fly around the world prize

STARTING TIPS

Create nine uncomfortable solutions to the problem at hand in two minutes and write these in the inner circles.

Select a number of these and try to develop nine ways to make each idea more acceptable. Record your ideas in the outer circles.

Then use the Four-step Speed Thinking Cycle to evaluate, build and action a number of the solutions.

Nine solutions that won't work

Another left-field application of *Speed Links* that seems counter-intuitive is to create a range of solutions that initially won't work.[5] Sometimes, to solve a problem in a non-linear way you have to use a non-linear process. In this case you deliberately create solutions that on the surface will fail. For example, it was only a few years ago that someone would have suggested 'Why don't we ask customers to serve themselves'. With this left-field solution, self-serve supermarkets developed and self check-in at airports has become common.

This thinking is particularly appropriate for the younger generation because through the use of technology anything seems possible. If it can be imagined, it can be built. Or as Don Tapscott observes, 'if video games taught this Net Generation anything, it's that every problem has seemingly endless solutions'.[6]

APPLICATION

Set yourself at least two minutes of uninterrupted thinking time. In the next two minutes, develop nine solutions to an everyday problem that you are sure won't work (remember not to filter) and write these in the inner circles. For example, if you are swamped with too much work, nine solutions that will not work might include: 'Take on a new project', 'Get rid of an employee', 'Advertise for more work', 'Bid for a new tender', 'Work even harder', 'Charge less'.

These are all solutions that on the surface seem to make the problem worse, but now comes the interesting part. Select one or more of the solutions at random and see if you can make it work. If I chose 'Advertise for more work' as an initial unworkable solution, I might try to turn this around by advertising for higher paid work, trying a brand image ad rather than a specific selling one, testing a new ad or a new placement in a magazine or newspaper, or trying to negotiate with the media agencies for a better advertising rate.

This is great fun in a group situation as well. You can pit one group against another, with one group designing seemingly unworkable solutions and challenging the other group to make these solutions viable. This process will ensure that you create a range of fresh, new solutions which can then be poured into the other steps of the Four-step Speed Thinking Cycle.

SPEED LINKS Challenge: ______________________________

Name: ______________________________ Date: ______________

Delegate more

Add more pressure

STARTING TIPS

In two minutes, create nine solutions to the problem that you are sure will *not* work and write these in the inner circles.

Select a number of these solutions and try to develop nine ways to make each solution work. Record your ideas in the outer circles.

CHAPTER 7

Nine ways to use *Speed Links* to fast-track your success

How would you use Speed Thinking in your life?

When managers of a major brand were asked how they would use Speed Thinking in their life, the most popular responses were:

1. To better manage my time
2. To solve everyday problems more quickly
3. To avoid procrastinating
4. To make faster decisions
5. To stop doubting myself
6. To avoid over-thinking simple things
7. To just go with an idea—just do it!
8. To stop wasting time so I can spend more time on important things
9. To get more things done

1 SPEED LINKS

What are my goals?

Setting formal or informal goals in our personal and work lives is the hallmark of most successful people. Sports psychologist Gayle Davis says, 'goal setting tells you where you need to go, how to get there, and when you are making progress. It encourages you to keep going'.[1]

So why don't more people set goals for themselves? Perhaps people enjoy drifting along. Perhaps they do not know how to set a clear goal (hint: think of using a SMART goal—one that is specific, measurable, attainable, realistic and timely).[2]

I suspect there are two other reasons. Firstly, we are all are time-poor. Sitting down to write a complex set of goals and action statements sounds like more hard work. People know they should, but they don't have the time. The second reason is that many of us tend to procrastinate. Setting a goal (e.g. to lose 2 kilos within three weeks) is something we can do tomorrow and we know that if we establish a goal and do not deliver on it, we risk failure—so why bother?

This *Speed Links* application can help on both counts. You can have a go at setting your goals in two minutes, so it is time-efficient, and because the process of setting goals is done quickly, you have no time to filter, so your authentic, deepest dreams may emerge.

APPLICATION

Have three *Speed Links* templates in front of you. In the next two minutes, develop nine long-term goals (e.g. what you want to achieve in the next 12 months). Then develop nine medium-term goals (e.g. what you want to achieve in the next three months) and finally nine short-term goals (e.g. what you want to achieve in the next week). Remember, the goals can be a mixture of business, financial, health, relationship and self-development and they must also fit within one another (i.e. short-term and medium-term goals are consistent with your long-term goals). Another variation is to develop nine usual goals and nine radical goals.

You may now have up to 27 goals. As quickly as you can, select three from each *Speed Links* and transfer these to a single *Speed Links* page. You will end up with all your goals on one piece of paper (or on a single screen on a computer).

SPEED LINKS Challenge: ______________________________

Name: ______________________________ Date: ____________

Cut out junk food

Become healthier

STARTING TIPS

Write 'Short-term goals' as the challenge at the top of the page. In two minutes, develop a series of goals and write them in the inner circles. (Repeat this for medium-term and long-term goals on separate Speed Links pages.)

Select your three most important short-term goals and, in the outside circles, write nine ways you are going to make these happen. (Repeat this for medium-term and long-term goals.) Combine these onto one *Speed Links* page.

What do we do next?

One of the major themes of this book is that we live in a world where 'more and more' is expected from us, while at the same time we have 'less and less' (i.e. time, money, budget and energy). With this variation of *Speed Links* I will show how you can use this tool to establish your priorities in a more efficient and productive way.

The essence of quicker thinking is simplicity. It seems to me that many time management systems become, in the end, too complex. The end point is completing a form correctly rather than helping you become better organised.

Sometimes we also feel overwhelmed by the demands in our lives. This is where *Speed Links* can help. It encourages you to get all your priorities down in a visual order, which makes it easier for you to rank your tasks and see how they all fit together.

APPLICATION

This application of *Speed Links* is a logical follow-on from the first. Once you have set your short-term, medium-term and long-term goals, you should be in a better position to establish your priorities.

Number the inner circles from 1 to 9.

Start by listing nine priorities in two minutes. Then score each priority from 1 to 10 in two minutes, according to its importance to you (10 being highly important, 1 not very important). Write the three top-scoring priorities in circles 1, 2 and 3, the next three in circles 4, 5 and 6, and so on.

Record progress against each priority in the outer circle.

Another way of handling your nine priorities is to score each priority from 1 to 10 in terms of how long it will take to do (the higher the score, the faster it can be done). This has an added advantage: when you think quickly you feel better, so it gives you an energy boost before moving on to the next priority.

Even better, you could give each priority an importance score and then a speed thinking score and add these together. The higher the scores, the higher the ranking. Using *Speed Links* in this way will ensure that you will always know what to do next!

SPEED LINKS Challenge: ______________________________

Name: ______________________________ Date: ____________

9.

8.

Put books away

1. Clean Office

STARTING TIPS

Write 'Priorities for this week' as the challenge at the top of the page. Then number each inner circle from 1 to 9.

List nine priorities in two minutes.

Now rank these priorities in terms of importance, speed or a combination of both (using a 1–10 scale).

Write these priorities in circles 1–9 according to your scores. Record progress against each priority in the outer circle.

7.

Called three prospects

2. Chase up new business

6.

3.

5.

4.

Resolve conflict quickly

This application of *Speed Links* encourages you to make explicit the thoughts, feelings and actions of yourself and others. By doing so you will gain a better insight into others' view of the world and it might help you to resolve conflict faster. It is important to try to capture what you imagine others might be thinking about a situation. As research psychologist Sarah Edelman notes, 'our thoughts influence the way that we feel and behave.'[3]

APPLICATION

Imagine that you are facing a difficult situation or something has happened that has left you feeling confused or upset. Try to capture the situation, dates and times (these are for your eyes only) in a *Speed Links* format.

The emphasis with this application is to jot down as quickly as you can (in the inner circles) what you are thinking and what the other person may be thinking about the same situation (perhaps five thoughts for you, four of the other person). For example, occasionally I argue with my teenage daughter and as a result I might capture these thoughts: 'Why does she raise her voice?', 'Why does she react so quickly?', 'I wish she would talk to me more', 'Why is she so aggressive?' I imagine she is probably thinking, 'Why is Dad picking on me again?', 'I can never please him', 'Does he love me?'

The aim is to capture these thoughts as quickly as possible and then to set these up visually across the *Speed Links*. Then select one thought and in the outer cricle create nine ways that would influence how you or the other person may feel or act. For example, the thought, 'Does he love me?' might lead to feelings of hurt, confusion, rejection, rebellion and actions of more arguing.

The next step is to try to develop nine approaches that can meet both points of view. This approach might lead to a faster and better resolution and will enable you to understand and be open to the views of others.

SPEED LINKS Challenge: ______________________________

Name: ______________________________ Date: ______________

STARTING TIPS

Write at the top of the page: the situation, the people involved and date (for your eyes only).

In two minutes, record in the inner circles your initial thoughts and also what the other person might be thinking about the situation.

Now select one of these thoughts and write in the outer circle nine feelings or actions that might flow from this thought.

In the connecting space, develop nine ways you might be able to resolve this situation for both parties.

How dare they challenge me?

I was right!

Frustration

I have more experience

What's holding you back?

Have you ever felt 'stuck' on a project that doesn't seem to be going anywhere? Perhaps your career or life more generally is at a crossroads and there seem to be all sorts of barriers stopping you from performing at your best? Any time you feel this way, this *Speed Links* application will prove helpful.

I believe in making any barriers or obstacles explicit. By doing so you focus your mind on exactly what the issue is and you can then discuss it with others if you wish. By making barriers explicit, it also feels as though you are proactively moving to overcome them.

Speed Thinking, with its emphasis on just starting without filtering and action, is an ideal way to quickly overcome any little barriers. These obstacles can be external (e.g. money) or internal (e.g. 'I could never do that, what if it fails?'). Speed Thinking provides you with a way to recognise these without dwelling on them. It can help you move forward and go around these 'speed bumps'.

APPLICATION

In the inner circles, write down as many obstacles that are holding you back as you can in two minutes. Then select one of these obstacles and in the outer circle suggest ways that you might overcome it. You might also randomly connect two of these obstacles and see if you can suggest ways to overcome both of them at the same time. For example, let's imagine that you are trying to get a new project approved. Some of the obstacles might be: budget, arranging a time to meet with your boss, the potential risks involved, limited people resources, your own workload. If you select one of these, the potential risks involved, ways to overcome this obstacle might include: looking for similar projects that might have worked, acknowledging the risks involved and what you are doing about them, showing lots of passion, looking to share the risk with another partner.

Another variation is to make the intangible barriers explicit (in two minutes) in the inner circle, then the external barriers explicit in the outer circle. If you are working in a group or project team, for example, you could create all the barriers to success quickly, then allocate one to a smaller group and ask them to see how they might overcome it. Then discuss and compare your responses.

SPEED LINKS Challenge: ______________________________

Name: ______________________________ Date: ______________

STARTING TIPS

In two minutes, write in the inner circles the barriers that are holding you back. These could be external (e.g. budget) or internal (e.g. unwillingness to take risks).

You could also create nine external barriers and nine internal barriers, then compare and contrast these.

Now select one or more of these inner circles and suggest nine ways to overcome it in the outer circle. Try to connect with another circle and see if your responses could overcome this obstacle as well.

What can I delegate?

My workload

Presentations—less is more!

In a time-poor world, the shorter the presentation the better—ideally, no more than nine slides. Why nine? Because our short-term memory is seven plus or minus two chunks of information. Sometimes even one slide is enough. In a recent Online Research Conference in the United Kingdom, there was a session called Ideas Rush. Participants were given five minutes and one slide to communicate a 'blazingly original idea'. The result? 'It's fast, furious and designed for delegates in search of bite-size inspiration.'[4]

APPLICATION

Speed Links can be used in a number of ways to enhance your fast-paced presentation. For example, you could plan your presentation with one key point in each of the inner circles. In the outer circles you could add support points. By planning in this way, you have a visual picture of your entire presentation and you can play around with the order of the slides.

You could also design a presentation that only takes nine minutes. It could be one slide or one key message per minute. This 'less is more'[5] approach is not only simpler and more time-efficient but paradoxically means that you have to be across your material even more. You can better engage and excite your audience with the thrill of a high-energy presentation. They will thank you by paying attention.

The advantage of using *Speed Links* is that you can prepare a better presentation in a shorter time and if you have only minutes it will force you to become more thorough and organised.

If you are working with a group or a partner, have each person capture what they believe are the most important points in two minutes. Then discuss and agree among the group what are the vital messages that the group has to communicate. This approach of starting with the individual and working up to the group is an ideal of way of harnessing what James Surowiecki calls 'the wisdom of crowds'.[6]

SPEED LINKS Challenge: ______________________________

Name: ______________________________ Date: ____________

STARTING TIPS

In two minutes, write in the inner circles the nine key points that you or your team want to make in the presentation. Try combining a number of bubbles and see what happens.

Reorder these points until you are happy with the flow.

In the outer circles, write any support points. In a few minutes you will have designed a compelling, easy-to-follow presentation.

What support do I need for this?

Introduce the central idea first

The Nine-minute Speed Meeting

A leader of a large bank recently bemoaned the snail pace of decision-making in business today. He observed that 'no one asks for a three-minute appointment, but there are plenty of two- to three-minute issues that you have to deal with'.[7] This comment made me think of a new way that leaders can meet with their team and make decisions—I have called it the Nine-minute Speed Meeting. It is a relatively formal meeting of nine minutes, with the following features:

- The location can be anywhere.
- The leader commits to nine minutes of undivided attention.
- The issue, challenge or decision must be an everyday one.
- There should be no more than three items.
- The decision must be able to be communicated in a few minutes and the leader then has at least one minute to decide or suggest a course of action.
- No notice is required of a nine-minute meeting other than the words 'Are you free to have a Speed Meeting?'
- No more than three or four people can attend.

The Speed Meeting means that you do not have to wait around for days or weeks on something that can be decided on immediately.

APPLICATION

I have based the Speed Meeting on Hudson's Law of Meetings, which states that the meeting expands to the set time. This is an adaptation of Parkinson's Law, which states that 'work expands so as to fill the time available for its completion'.[8]

The *Speed Links* tool is an ideal way to organise a Speed Meeting. If you are preparing for this meeting, list all the everyday decisions that need to be made in the inner circles. Now organise these thoughts from 1 to 9 in order of how quickly the decision can be made. The fastest decisions are to go first. This will create movement and energy in the meeting. Record the decisions in the outer circles.

As with the entire Speed Thinking concept, the Nine-minute Speed Meeting enhances and complements existing meetings rather than replacing them.

SPEED LINKS Challenge: ______________________________

Name: ______________________________ Date: ______________

STARTING TIPS

In two minutes, write in the inner circles the nine key day-to-day decisions you need your boss to make.

Number these from 1 to 9 in order of how quickly these decisions can be made.

In the outer circles, write down the decisions made.

Yes!

Can we have a mufti day on Friday?

Improve your study and exam results

At the time of writing, my eldest daughter is sitting her final school exams. These will determine to a large extent if she is fortunate enough to be accepted into university. It is a stressful time as she tries to ensure that she is across all the required content.

Teachers at her school do a wonderful job in helping her to prepare by reviewing past papers. However, they are not quite as successful in giving her the tools to do the exam on the day. Certainly, students must know the material, but sometimes they can freeze, or have a mental block or find it difficult to get started. This is where Speed Thinking could be of enormous help. By its very nature, it enables anyone to think quickly under time pressure—the very definition of most exams. *Speed Links* can help by providing students with a valuable tool to start building a more interesting, original and complete essay. It does this by helping them to remember, access and connect information quickly.

APPLICATION

The design of the *Speed Links* tool can help students to take notes and to better recall these. Because there are nine circles this works within our short memory capacity (i.e. seven plus or minus two). It forces students to have one core thought and a number of associations (i.e. chunking). For example, if you try to remember the numbers 713895231, it is difficult. However, if you group these into 71 38 95 23 1, it is much easier. There is also some evidence that when we use all our senses to link items together we are better at remembering these.[9]

You can use *Speed Links* to capture notes (e.g. core points in the inner circles and related minor points in the outer circles), to study (use the same approach) and in exams. In a high-pressure situation like an exam, it is important not to panic. A student can draw up the *Speed Links* design (if they are not allowed to take it into an exam) and capture nine central points of an essay, for example, then the related points. They can also try to connect the bubbles to make additional points. Don't worry about the order in which you capture the key points, as you can rearrange these later.

SPEED LINKS Challenge: ____________________

Name: ____________________ Date: __________

STARTING TIPS

In an exam situation, quickly write in the inner circles nine key points of an essay.

Then write down nine related points in the outer circles.

Then look to connect the circles to build extra points.

Now order each of the circles from 1 to 9. Each of these may form the basis of a paragraph or you can combine them. You have now structured your entire essay.

Secondary points are . . .

The author's main point is . . .

Exercise your brain and keep young

One of the main findings of the recent surge in brain research is that 'the human brain can change itself'.[10] By this, the brain researchers mean that each of us has a wonderful capacity to continually learn and grow throughout our life. But there is a catch. We need to take responsibility for nourishing and maintaining a rich mental life. Not only will we lead more productive lives but, according to neuroscientist Michael Valenzuela, 'individuals with higher levels of lifetime mental activity had a 46 per cent lower chance of developing dementia'.[11]

The lesson? As John Medina comments, 'the brain is like a muscle. The more activity you do, the more experience you have, the larger and more complex the brain becomes.'[12]

Speed Thinking, with its emphasis on creating movement, ideas, solutions and energy, is an ideal way to exercise your brain. Speed Thinking is both enjoyable and challenging and has the added advantages that it is simple, intuitive and fun.

APPLICATION

According to Ryuta Kawashima, 'solving simple calculations quickly is the most effective way of activating your brain'.[13] If this is the case, Speed Thinking might be another useful way of lighting up your brain.

I would like to invite you to use *Speed Links* in any way that can help you—to remember your shopping list or decide where to eat out at night, for example. By using Speed Thinking daily, you can create a new idea, solve a problem or make a decision and you exercise your brain.

If you are a parent, *Speed Links* is a tool that you could share with your kids. You could have races as to who might be the first to solve a common problem. For example, 'What could we as a family do this Sunday?' Each person suggests an option and these are recorded in the inner circles. Then you select a couple of options and in the outer circles record ways to make them nine times better, or you might connect a few (e.g. 'We could catch a ferry over to the zoo').

SPEED LINKS **Challenge:** ______________________________

Name: ______________________________ **Date:** __________

STARTING TIPS

In the inner circles, have each family member write down their solution to a common challenge as fast as they can.

Then select a few and use the outer circles to make these solutions nine times better, or try to connect a few of the solutions (in two minutes each).

Let's have Thai food!

Let's eat out tonight

Feel more energised right now!

Speed Thinking is a powerful adaptation to an accelerating world. As Vince Poscente suggests, 'when we harness the power of speed, we not only get more and get it faster, but our lives and work become less stressful, less busy and more balanced'.[14] Research by Emily Pronin and Elana Jacobs suggests that thinking quickly has the added advantage of triggering an almost immediate lift in mood.[15]

Thinking quickly also greatly expands your possibilities by blocking your often critical internal voice. As brain scientist and stroke victim Jill Bolte Taylor insightfully notes, 'many of us spend an inordinate amount of time and energy degrading, insulting and criticising ourselves (and others) for having made a wrong or bad decision. When you berate yourself, have you ever questioned who inside of you is doing the yelling, and at whom are you yelling?'[16] With Speed Thinking you have no time to listen to this little voice because you are too busy creating, solving, deciding or just being. Your original, authentic self emerges.

APPLICATION

I believe that the trick to feeling energised right now is not to over-think things. The problem with having too much time in a particular situation seems to be that your conscious, analytical mind tries to plan and control your actions in advance. You tend to remind yourself of everything that can go wrong. This often leads to indecision and hesitation.

Speed Thinking keeps you in the here and now. You are too busy to worry about the past or to get too far ahead of yourself in the future. As psychologist and therapist Richard Carlson suggests, 'a genuinely happy person knows that life is nothing more than a constant series of present moments to be experienced, one right after another. They strive to experience each present moment of their lives to the fullest.'[17]

With this application of *Speed Links*, every now and then write down nine good things about your life in two minutes, or nine things that you feel passionate about or nine things you would love to do in the next ten years. Keep this to yourself or discuss with your partner. It will make you feel energised every moment of the day.

SPEED LINKS Challenge: ______________________________

Name: ______________________________ Date: ______________

STARTING TIPS

In two minutes, write in the inner circles nine things that make you smile.

Then select a few and write in the outer circle nine specific actions that you can take to experience more of this thing (two minutes each).

Pick them up from school

Spending time with my kids

CHAPTER 8

The most commonly asked questions about Speed Thinking

'What would you do if you weren't afraid?'

Spencer Johnson, *Who Moved My Cheese?*

Here are answers to some of the most commonly asked questions about Speed Thinking.

What was the insight behind Speed Thinking?

The insight for Speed Thinking came from my workshops with business people and my graduate students. In attempting to work through more material, I kept giving participants in my workshops less and less time to complete a task. Paradoxically, this seemed to have no detrimental effect on the quality of their performance. In fact, the originality of their responses appeared to be enhanced. I was intrigued by this phenomenon and wondered what the natural limit might be.

Through trial and error, I have discovered that if you set participants an everyday challenge, with a two-minute time limit, and you ask them to create at least nine different responses, then magic happens. My theory is that, because people are moving so quickly, they do not filter their responses or worry about the expectations of others and operate at what I call the 'edge of their unconscious'.

How does Speed Thinking compare with traditional thinking?

A good way of visualising the answer to this question is the yin–yang symbol. In Chinese philosophy, yin–yang is used to describe how seemingly opposing forces are interconnected and interdependent in the natural world, giving rise to each other in turn. In a similar way, Speed Thinking (yang) provides energy, movement and acceleration, while traditional thinking (yin) encourages a more disciplined, critical and reflective approach. For example, have you ever been struggling with a problem (yin) and in an instant a new solution emerges (yang)?

Both ways of thinking are necessary and together make up an effective total thinking approach. You can select either approach depending on the situation, time available and your personal preference. Or you can use these in combination, much like going for a run where you can walk, jog or sprint in any order.

My suggestion is to give Speed Thinking a go today. It can help you make a day-to-day decision, create an idea or solve a problem quickly with no reduction in quality. In fact, because you do not filter your responses, your results can improve. You will also feel better and you can contemplate all you want after you have acted.

Research bites

Researchers Charles Limb and Allen Braun, in an ingenious study, asked six highly trained jazz musicians to play a keyboard while in the confines of an MRI. They found that, 'during improvisation, the brain deactivates the area involved in self-monitoring and observation, while cranking up the region linked with self expression'.

'Essentially a musician shuts down his/her inhibitions and lets their inner voice shine through,' Limb explains.

Nick Zagorski, 'Music on the mind', Hopkins Medicine Magazine Online Version, Spring/Summer, 2008

Can you really have too much time to think?

Many people complain to me that they do not have enough time to think. 'If only I had more time, I could create a better idea or solution', they suggest. Perhaps this is true, but do we ever suffer from the opposite problem? Can we have too much time to think? I was reminded of this when a commentator at the Australian Tennis Open suggested that, because the second serve of a player was slow, it meant the receiving player had too much time to think and as a result was losing their rhythm.

In the sporting arena, the problem with having too much time seems to be that your conscious, analytical mind tries to plan and control your actions in advance and you remind yourself of all that can go wrong. This often leads to indecision and hesitation. Should I go for the top left-hand corner of the net when taking the penalty kick or should I wait for the goalkeeper to commit? Maybe I should keep it low? What if I miss? These thoughts swirl around and it is no wonder that many soccer coaches suggest that you should commit to one spot and just kick the ball.

It is a paradox, but having too much time can make you less efficient. I have noticed the same pattern with business people. After an exhaustive analysis, managers can tell you everything that can go wrong with any number of options, which in the end means that they do not try anything. This might be the worst option of all, as nothing will stop the more nimble, flexible competitor.

Having too much time is just one example of a thinking error that we all suffer from. My concept of Speed Thinking is just one way to overcome this self-limiting barrier. The aim of Speed Thinking is to encourage people to just do—to create and select an option that feels right at the time and completely commit to it.

Is speed thinking the same as intuition?

Speed Thinking shares many of the qualities of intuition:

- Both are modes of quick thought. In fact, intuition is almost instantaneous.
- Both are right-brain processes. I would also argue that Speed Thinking is more about accessing the unconscious and intuition the emotions.
- Both benefit through experiential learning (i.e. you get better at both the more experience you have).
- Both modes of thought are often viewed with some suspicion by rational business people as compromising quality—even though there is plenty of evidence that people rely on intuition a great deal when making decisions.

But there are differences:

- Intuition is more of an internal process, Speed Thinking an external one.
- Intuition is more individual. Speed Thinking is both an individual and a group process. It can be used in meetings, for example.
- Intuition is typically used by someone who has a particular (often extensive) expertise and experience, whereas Speed Thinking can be used by anyone, of any age, in any role, with little or no experience.
- Intuition is mainly used for decision-making. Speed Thinking can be used to create new ideas, solve problems and make decisions.
- Intuition is difficult to teach, whereas Speed Thinking (I believe) fits easily into an educational mode because of its four-step process (Start, Evaluate, Build, Action), two-minute, nine-possibility mechanic and the range of *Speed Links* applications.

In short, Speed Thinking is a more structured, external, tool-driven process than intuition.

>> *'The creative is the place where no one else has ever been.*
> *You have to leave the city of your comfort and go into the wilderness of your intuition.*
> *What you'll discover will be wonderful.*
> *What you'll discover is yourself.'*
>
> Alan Alda, actor

Is Speed Thinking the same as lateral thinking or brainstorming?

The father of lateral thinking, Edward de Bono, has made a wonderful contribution to our understanding of how our brain might work. His concept that the brain acts like a self-organising, information patterning system was way ahead of its time.

But is lateral thinking (i.e. deliberately moving across a pattern) enough in this fast-paced world?

My proposition is that both critical and creative thinking, while necessary, are not sufficient any more. We need to be able to think and act faster. This will enable us to better thrive in an accelerating and time-poor world.

I have tried to build on de Bono's work by adding an extra dimension. We can now control not only how we think but at what pace we think. And by doing so we can become more creative, efficient, productive and energised.

How can I improve my Speed Thinking?

Speed Thinking, like any other skill, can be improved with practice, using some of the tools suggested in this book, following the two-minute, nine-possibility challenge and some perseverance. It is a thinking system built on just starting and moving forward. The important point is to try Speed Thinking and see if it works for you. You can select when and how to use it depending on the time available, nature of the problem or personal preference.

When should you not use Speed Thinking?

As a general rule, I would not use Speed Thinking on those life-turning decisions where analysis and reflection are vital. Speed Thinking is specifically designed to be used for everyday problems, challenges or decisions. It is ideal for time-pressure situations when you just have to produce a result quickly, for example, in an exam.

Research bites

Research by Ap Dijksterhuis and Teun Meurs in experiments with students found that unconscious thought is an active process that enables you to be more associative, divergent and creative.

A. Dijksterhuis and T. Meurs, 'Where creativity resides: The generative power of unconscious thought', *Consciousness and Cognition*, vol. 15, 2006, pp. 135–46.

Doesn't quality suffer when you think quickly?

No. Speed Thinking complements but does not replace traditional thinking. Some problems or decisions need to be analysed and reflected upon. However, many day-to-day challenges can be handled in a fast way without compromising quality. In fact, Speed Thinking, with its initial emphasis on not restricting options and then evaluating them, can lead to stronger ideas, solutions and decisions. Its iterative nature means that if you reach a roadblock, you simply go back and start again. The most you lose is two minutes.

I have also found that the accessibility and fun of Speed Thinking create a situation where more people can become better thinkers and certainly are more open to the ideas of others.

How does Speed Thinking fit with time-management courses?

Remember when time-management courses were all the rage? They seemed to make perfect sense. There were courses on managing staff, managing projects and managing budgets, so the idea of a course on managing time was the next logical step. You apply the same rational approach that you do to every other business activity. You plan, control, prioritise, review, and so on. But is this the way that we should be thinking about time?

I believe we have entered a new era where so much (e.g. work, growth, sales, information) is expected from so few resources (e.g. time, people, dollars) that trying to become better at managing time will not be enough. Being able to prioritise the most important tasks is necessary, but in my view not sufficient.

My aim with Speed Thinking is to help everyone create more time for themselves by becoming more efficient and productive with everyday problems, ideas and solutions. By doing so, you also feel better and improve your productivity. Importantly, you can free up more time to invest in other activities that have meaning to you.

The thrust of Speed Thinking is that everyday problems can be resolved by not over-thinking these—by keeping it simple and by thinking more quickly. All you need is two minutes and the courage not to filter your responses. It is not about managing time but creating more of it for you to spend how you wish.

Research bites

Research by Kalina Christoff, Alan Gordon and Rachelle Smith suggests that spontaneous thoughts (i.e. day-dreaming or mind-wandering) display the following characteristics:

- The brain regions recruited during spontaneous thinking overlap with those recruited during goal-directed thought.
- Spontaneous thought competes for brain capacity with goal-directed thought processes.
- Our capacity for spontaneous thought increases during highly practised tasks.
- It decreases with age.

Kalina Christoff, Alan Gordon and Rachelle Smith, 'The role of spontaneous thought in human cognition', in O. Vartanian and D.R. Mandel (eds), *Neuroscience of Decision Making*, Psychology Press, New York, 2008.

Can you measure the impact of Speed Thinking?

I surveyed my graduate students at the University of Technology, Sydney, on the effects of my work.

I asked each of my students in an elective subject called Marketing Creativity to rate how fast they were as a thinker at the beginning of the course on a ten-point scale (1 being very slow, 10 extremely fast). Their average score was 4.61. After approximately five hours (i.e. ten sessions of 30 minutes) training in Speed Thinking, I asked the students again and their score (on average) increased to 6.63—an increase of 44 per cent!

I put the increase down to three main factors. Talking about Speed Thinking raised the students' consciousness of it. They also became more confident thinking quickly because they practised it each week. Finally, I gave them a range of tools that seemed to increase their speed and confidence. They could choose ones that suited their personal preferences.

A quick result: 110 ideas in two minutes rather than 14!

I recently conducted a Speed Thinking session with a large organisation and was explaining the difference between the traditional brainstorming method and a Speed Thinking version.

I asked the participants to describe a problem that they were struggling with and divided the larger group into smaller groups. Each group then tackled the problem using the old approach (i.e. one person capturing the ideas as people call these out). The highest number of ideas in a group was fourteen in a five-minute period.

I then asked people to use the Speed Thinking approach to the same problem (i.e. each person works by themselves and tries to create nine possibilities in two minutes). Using this approach, the same group created 110 ideas in two minutes—almost an eight times increase! There was some duplication of ideas, but the difference in output was profound. In addition, everyone was more involved and energised.

Are extroverts better at Speed Thinking than introverts?

It is too early to judge whether or not this is the case because the concept of Speed Thinking is still so new. However, in some of my workshops I gained a few tentative insights.

The concept of Speed Thinking seems to be more easily embraced by extroverts than introverts. They seem to enjoy the concept, it energises and excites them.

Introverts, by comparison, feel slightly uncomfortable with the concept of reacting too quickly. They like to consider, internalise and deliberate on their responses. However, I have found that for these people a little encouragement to stay with the process can pay dividends.

There is some support for this finding in the literature. For example, David Rawlings and Debbie Carnie found that on measures of intelligence, extroverts performed better than introverts under timed task conditions.

> *'I have taken two minutes out to write and thank you for your Speed Thinking workshop. Here are nine reasons why I enjoyed it:*
>
> 1. *It was fun.*
> 2. *The tools are invaluable.*
> 3. *It made me think differently.*
> 4. *It was a good networking opportunity.*
> 5. *The interactive exercises were good.*
> 6. *It provided me with insight.*
> 7. *It challenged my existing way of thinking.*
> 8. *It refocused me.*
> 9. *The view was amazing!'*
>
> Julie Tyson, telecommunications manager

Can Speed Thinking help people with depression?

Recent research by Emily Pronin and others has confirmed that thinking more quickly can have a positive impact on your mood and leave you feeling more energised.[2] I have found exactly the same effect in my Speed Thinking sessions. Both the people in my workshop (and myself) have experienced this great burst of energy where anything seems possible.

A friend of mine suffers from mild depression and has recently been using Speed Thinking to help him cope. John (not his real name) reports that using Speed Thinking gives him a feeling of accomplishment. It enables him to make a decision or solve a problem or create a new idea quickly. The process of thinking quickly makes him feel good immediately and he can see the result of what he was doing (e.g. meeting his girlfriend for a surprise lunch), which makes him feel more in control of his life and gives him a greater sense of achievement.

John uses Speed Thinking for the smaller things in his life and he feels that this gives him momentum and confidence to tackle the bigger things.

I did not initially design Speed Thinking for use in the treatment of depression, but perhaps it can help certain people deal with this illness and lead more productive and fulfilling lives.

> *'We cannot resist the speculation that happiness exercises may prove therapeutic in depressive disorders.*
>
> *It is important to note that these interventions also reduced depressive symptoms lastingly, and in other studies we are finding that this effect is massive.'*
>
> Martin Seligman, Nansook Park and Christopher Peterson, 'Positive psychology progress'

For more information about Speed Thinking visit:
www.thespeedthinkingzone.com

Notes

INTRODUCTION

1. A. Dijksterhuis, M.W. Bos, L.G. Nordgren, and R.B. Van Baaren, 'On making the right choice: The deliberation without attention effect', *Science,* vol. 311, 17 February 2006.
2. M. Gladwell, *Blink: The power of thinking without thinking,* Allen Lane, Camberwell, Victoria, 2005.

CHAPTER 1

1. Source: Wikipedia.
2. V. Poscente, *The Age of Speed: Learning to thrive in a more-faster-now world,* Ballantine Books, New York, 2008, p. 45.
3. D. Tapscott, *Grown Up Digital: How the net generation is changing your world,* McGraw Hill, New York, 2009, p. 93.
4. Commissioned by Robert Hall Technology, October 2008.

5. J.A. Babraj, V. Niels, C. Keast, F.M. Guppy, C. Cottrell and J.A. Timmons, BMC Endocrine Disorders, vol. 9, no. 3, 2009, available at <www.biomedcentral.com>.

CHAPTER 2

1. My PhD thesis was 'Designing a continuously creative organisation', University of Western Sydney, 2001.
2. G. Winter, *High Performance Leadership*, John Wiley & Sons, Singapore, 2003, p. 43.
3. M. Csikszentmihalyi, *Creativity: Flow and the psychology of discovery and invention*, Harper Perennial, New York, 1996.
4. E. Pronin and E. Jacobs, 'Thought speed, mood and the experience of mental motion', *Perspectives on Psychological Science*, vol. 3, 2008, pp. 461–85.
5. This concept of enjoying a high-arousal experience is similar to Michael Apter's Reversal Theory; see M.J. Apter, *Motivational Styles in Everyday Life: A guide to reversal theory*, American Psychological Association, Washington D.C.
6. R. Marois and P. Dux, 'Multi-tasking ability can be improved through training', Vanderbilt University, *ScienceDaily*, 27 July 2009.
7. B. Rotella, *Your 15th Club*, Free Press, New York, p. 94.
8. W.T. Gallwey, *The Inner Game of Golf*, Random House, London, 1981, p. 33.
9. S.L. Brown, and K.M. Eisenhardt, *Competing on the Edge*, Harvard Business School Press, Boston, MA, 1998, p. 28.
10. See, for example, T.D. Wilson, *Strangers to Ourselves: Discovering the adaptive unconscious*, Harvard College, Cambridge, MA, 2002.
11. K. Christoff, A. Gordon and R. Smith, 'The role of spontaneous thought in human cognition', in O. Vartanian and D.R. Mandel (eds), *Neuroscience of Decision Making*, Psychology Press, New York, 2009.

CHAPTER 3

1. B. Goodwin, *How the Leopard Changed its Spots: The evolution of complexity*, Phoenix Publishing, London, 1997, p. 179.

2. M. Hewitt-Gleeson, *Software for the Brain 2*, Wrightbooks, North Brighton, Victoria, 1991, p. 17.
3. R. Carlson, *Stop Thinking, Start Living*, Harper Collins Publishing, London, 2003, p. 25.
4. T.D. Wilson and J.W. Schooler, 'Thinking too much: Introspection can reduce the quality of preferences and decisions', *Journal of Personality and Social Psychology*, vol. 60, no. 2, February 1991, pp. 181–92.
5. Christine Canabou, *Fast Ideas for Slow Times*, Fast Company, New York, 19 December 2007.

CHAPTER 4

1. K. Hudson, *The Idea Generator*, Allen & Unwin, Sydney, 2007, pp. vii–xvi.
2. K. Hudson, 'Designing a continuously creative organisation', University of Western Sydney, 2001.
3. The emphasis on selecting initial thoughts at random is adapted from the work of Edward de Bono and his insight that our minds work as a self-organising information patterning system. See, for example, E. de Bono, *Serious Creativity: Using the power of lateral thinking to create new ideas*, Harper Collins, London, 1992.
4. R. Lowe, *Improvisation, Inc.: Harnessing spontaneity to engage people and groups,* Jossey-Bass/Pfeiffer, San Francisco, 2000, pp. 47–50.
5. This is similar to the ideas of W.T. Gallwey; see W.T. Gallwey, *The Inner Game of Work*, Texere Publishing, New York, 2000.

CHAPTER 5

1. For a wonderful read on many case studies of people who use their intuition, or what Malcolm Gladwell calls 'thin slicing', see M. Gladwell, *Blink: The power of thinking without thinking*, Penguin, Victoria, 2005.
2. Research by Kathleen Eisenhardt suggests that in fast-moving environments faster decision-making is associated with better performance because it enables leaders to keep pace with the competition and take advantage of opportunities and leads to faster learning. K.M. Eisenhardt, 'Making fast strategic decisions

in high velocity environments', *Academy of Management Journal*, 1989, vol. 32, no. 3, pp. 543–76.

3. A.R. Damasio, *Descartes' Error: Emotion, reason and the human brain*, Papermac, London, 1996, p. xv.
4. J. Lehrer, *The Decisive Moment*, Text Publishing, Melbourne, 2009, p. 5.
5. J. Welch, *Jack: What I've Learned Leading a Great Company and Great People*, Headline Book Publishing, London, 2001, p. 398.
6. R. Branson, *Screw It, Let's Do It*, Random House, Australia, 2006, p. 56.
7. T. Gura, 'I'll do it tomorrow', *Scientific American Mind*, Dec. 2008–Jan. 2009, pp. 27–31.
8. A.P. Dijksterhuis, M.W. Bos, L.G. Nordgren and R.B. Van Baaren, 'On making the right choice: The deliberation without attention effect', *Science*, vol. 311, 17 February 2006.

CHAPTER 6

1. G. Klein, *The Power of Intuition: How to use your gut feelings to make better decisions at work*, Doubleday Publishers, New York, 2004, p. 25.
2. J. Kounios, J. Fleck, D.L. Green, L. Payne, J.L. Stevenson, M. Bowden and M. Jung-Beeman, 'The origins of insight in resting state brain activity', *Neuropsychologia*, vol. 46, pp. 281–91, 2008.
3. This application is also covered in K. Hudson, *The Idea Generator*, Allen & Unwin, Sydney, 2007, pp. 16–17.
4. This application is also covered in K. Hudson, *The Idea Generator*, pp. 6–7.
5. This application is also covered in K. Hudson, *The Idea Generator*, pp. 18–19.
6. D. Tapscott, *Grown Up Digital: How the net generation is changing your world*, McGraw Hill, New York, 2009, p. 168.

CHAPTER 7

1. G.A. Davis, *High Performance Thinking*, Psychology Connections, Colorado Springs, 1999, p. 59.
2. The first use of the term is unknown, but Peter Drucker, in his 1954 seminal work *The Practice of Management*, outlined a system

that was very similar to SMART objectives while discussing objective-based management.

3. S. Edelman, *Change Your Thinking*, ABC Books, Sydney, 2001, p. 6.
4. As advertised by the UK-based *Research* magazine for an Online Research Conference held on 30 August 2009.
5. 'Less is more' is a quote from Ludwig Mies van der Rohe, architect and leader of the Bauhaus movement in Germany.
6. J. Surowiecki, *The Wisdom of Crowds: Why the many are smarter than the few and how collective wisdom shapes business, economies, societies and nations*, Little, Brown, New York, 2004.
7. Interview in *The Australian*, 24 June 2009, p. 19.
8. Adapted from Cyril Northcote Parkinson, who suggested in 1955 (in a tongue-in-cheek way) what has since become known as Parkinson's Law. It states: 'Work expands so as to fill the time available for its completion.'
9. T. Buzan, *Make the Most of your Mind*, Simon & Schuster, New York, 1988, p. 45. For an easy read on improving your memory, see G.G. Scott, *30 Days to a More Powerful Memory*, AMACOM Books, New York, 2007.
10. N. Doidge, *The Brain that Changes Itself*, Scribe Publications, Melbourne, 2007, p. xiii.
11. M.J. Valenzuela, a review of 22 studies and 29,000 individuals over an average of seven years: *It's never too late to change your mind*, ABC Books, Sydney, 2009, p. 163.
12. J.J. Medina, 'The science of thinking smarter: A conversation with brain expert John J. Medina', *Harvard Business Review*, May 2008, pp. 51–4.
13. R. Kawashima, *Train Your Brain*, Penguin Books, London, 2007, p. 6.
14. V. Poscente, *The Age of Speed*, Ballantine Books, New York, 2008, p. 5.
15. E. Pronin and E. Jacobs, 'Thought speed, mood and the experience of mental motion', *Perspectives on Psychological Science*, vol. 3, 2008, pp. 461–85.
16. J.B. Taylor, *My Stroke of Insight: A brain scientist's personal journey*, Hodder & Stoughton, London, 2008, p. 138.

17. R. Carlson, *Stop Thinking, Start Living*, Element Publishing, London, 2003, p. 105.

CHAPTER 8

1. D. Rawlings and D. Carnie, 'The interaction of EPQ extra version with WAIS subtest performance under timed and untimed conditions', *Personality and Individual Differences*, vol. 10, no. 4, 1989, pp. 453–8.
2. E. Pronin and D.M. Wegner, 'Manic thinking: Independent effects of thought speed and thought content on mood', *Psychological Science*, vol. 17, 2006, pp. 807–13.

Further reading

Buzan, T., *Make the Most of Your Mind,* Simon & Schuster, New York, 1988

Carlson, R., *Stop Thinking, Start Living*, Element Publishing, London, 2003

Csikszentmihalyi, M., *Creativity: Flow and the psychology of discovery and invention,* Harper Perennial, New York, 1996

De Bono, E., *Serious Creativity: Using the power of lateral thinking to create new ideas,* Harper Collins, London, 1992

Doidge, N., *The Brain that Changes Itself,* Scribe Publications, Melbourne, 2007

Edelman, S., *Change your Thinking*, ABC Books, Sydney, 2001

Gallwey, W.T., *The Inner Game of Golf,* Random House, London, 1981

Gladwell, M., *Blink: The power of thinking without thinking*, Allen Lane, Camberwell, Victoria, 2005

Hewitt-Gleeson, M., *Software for the Brain 2,* Wrightbooks, North Brighton, Victoria, 1991

Hudson, K., *The Idea Generator*, Allen & Unwin, Sydney, 2007

Hudson, K., *The Idea Accelerator*, Allen & Unwin, Sydney, 2008
Kawashima, R., *Train Your Brain*, Penguin Books, London, 2007
Klein, G., *The Power of Intuition: How to use your gut feelings to make better decisions at work*, Doubleday Publishers, New York, 2004
Poscente, V., *The Age of Speed*, Ballantine Books, New York, 2008
Surowiecki, J., *The Wisdom of Crowds: Why the many are smarter than the few and how collective wisdom shapes business, economies, societies and nations*, Little, Brown, New York, 2004
Taylor, L.B., *My Stroke of Insight: A brain scientist's personal journey*, Hodder & Stoughton, London, 2008
Valenzuela M.J., *It's Never Too Late to Change Your Mind*, ABC Books, Sydney, 2009
Wilson, T.D., *Strangers to Ourselves: Discovering the adaptive unconscious*, Harvard College, Cambridge, MA, 2002

Speed Thinking Templates

SPEED LINKS Challenge: ______________________________

Name: ______________________________ Date: ______________

SPEED LINKS Challenge: ______________________________

Name: ______________________________ Date: ____________

SPEED LINKS Challenge: ____________________

Name: ____________________ Date: __________

SPEED LINKS Challenge: ______________________________

Name: ______________________________ Date: ____________

SPEED LINKS Challenge: ______________________________

Name: ______________________________ Date: ____________

SPEED LINKS Challenge: ______________________________

Name: ______________________________ Date: ____________

SPEED LINKS Challenge: ______________________________

Name: ______________________________ Date: ______________

SPEED LINKS Challenge: ______________________________

Name: ______________________________ Date: ____________

SPEED LINKS Challenge: ______________________

Name: ______________________ Date: __________